Peace of Body

Peace of Mind

D0556664

PRACTICAL, EFFECTIVE TECHNIQUES
FOR
MENTAL FITNESS

Rose VanSickle

Grateful acknowledgement is made for permission to reprint *Let There Be Peace On Earth* by Jan-Lee Music, © 1955, © renewed 1983. Reprinted by permission of Janet Taché.

Author's note:
The methods and ideas presented in this book are not intended as a replacement for consulting a mental health professional. All conditions regarding your health require professional direction.

The purpose of this book is to educate. If you do not wish to be bound by the above, you may return this book to the publisher for a full refund.

Cover design by Susan Powers.
Printed in the United States of America.
Third printing - 2002

Published by:
PLJ Unlimited, Inc.
P.O. Box 98441
Raleigh, NC 27624-8441
www.pljunlimited.com

A portion of the profits of this book will be donated to Recovery, Inc.®

ISBN 0-9649506-1-8

Library of Congress Catalog Card Number: 95-92855

Acknowledgements

*I want to thank my **Support Team**, the friends and guides, who gave willingly and lovingly to help make this book a reality. You have been generous with light, love, financial support, encouragement and enthusiasm. I thank each and every one of you. Your support will reach millions.*

—— Rose

For Sarah

This book is dedicated to

You.

Peace, Love & Joy

Rose

Contents

Part Five-Eliminating Core Stressors

Part Six - Unlocking Limits

Introduction

Experiencing *Peace of Body and Peace of Mind* means feeling calm and alive, and good about yourself. With inner calm you feel better physically and mentally, you have a sense of vitality. Without inner calm you are a victim of nervous tension, struggle and inner turmoil. The purpose of this book is to teach you *how* to feel and be more calm. The methods presented go beyond coping with stress and strain. You will learn to *identify* the true source of your tension and *what to do* to *eliminate* that source. Your mind and body will be more comfortable and at ease.

You do not have to go through life feeling anxious, depressed or upset. Peace and contentment ARE within your reach. The personal management skills presented in this book will teach you new ways to think and act. No matter how you feel, your feelings and difficulties are not unique. Inner calm and composure are possible. There are time-proven techniques to create peace from the inside-out. Whether your exploration has just begun, or you have spent years searching for an inner sense of calm, YOUR life can be better.

You CAN erase stress in your daily life and cope with routine frustrations. You CAN combat the feeling of being overwhelmed and purge yourself of hurt and resentment. You CAN eliminate the tension, the cause of physical or emotional wear and tear, and the effects, the acid stomach, tightness in the back of your neck, headaches, the general feeling of uneasiness. You CAN cancel negative feelings that cause you to wake up dreading the day and most of the tasks on your agenda. If you are plagued with an attitude even you don't want to live with, you CAN change your outlook and free yourself of irritable, cranky or overreactive behavior.

● Did you believe your life would be easier and more pleasant once you reached a certain age and started making your own decisions? Is being an adult not quite as satisfying as you thought it would be? Are you disappointed, discouraged, disillusioned or disgusted?

- Do you listen to people who claim to be their own best friend and know you would love to be in the same frame of mind? Are you frustrated, confused and annoyed because no one ever taught you the art of self-acceptance?
- Have you ever wished you could "trade your life in for a new one?" If life had a money-back guarantee, would you have already requested your refund?
- Are you on a spiritual path striving to drop the judgement which is blocking your growth? Intellectually, you know forgiveness is the key and negative thoughts stifle growth, but do you still lack sound guidance on "how to" affect a transformation?
- If you carry the label of an emotional, nervous or mental disorder, your inner voice only speaks of "doom and gloom." No one needs to point out that your negative thoughts outweigh your positive thoughts. Are you still waiting for practical direction as to "how" you are supposed to recondition your life?

Reaching a level of inner contentment is not a matter of empowerment, a power furnished to you from an outside source. It is "in-powerment," an inner strength *you* develop once you are provided with the correct information. Using this Method will take you from merely existing, to living a fuller life. It will free you from the endless loop of, "I want to... But how?"

I have *lived* the techniques in this book for more than a decade. They have lifted me from a life of crises to a life of calm; from inner chaos to confidence, courage and composure. The techniques have taken me from illness to high-level wellness; from an inner-being racked with fear and frustration to a person with poise and power. They have liberated me from a life of stress and pain, to a peaceful existence. My negative belief system has been replaced by inner strength.

This work is based on the knowledge I gained through Recovery, Inc.,® a self-help, mental fitness system. It is about the program's techniques and beliefs, as I understand them, and how I adapted them into my daily life. This is my tribute to the late Abraham A. Low, M.D., the man whose insight, caring, wisdom and devotion created this program for inner-healing. I have been sharing my experience with people for years. Through this book, I am able to communicate the rewards of Dr. Low's Method to a wider audience.

Recovery, Inc. is NOT about substance abuse and addiction. The program was born in 1937, long before "recovery" became a generic term in addiction treatment. It is a set of essential, stress-reducing life skills that teach you *how* to achieve peace and contentment. Its' focus is wellness and wholeness and it nurtures the most important person in your life—YOU.

This book presents practical techniques to overcome the negatives that rob your inner peace. The wellness system offers powerful solutions whether you suffer mild, moderate, chronic or severe emotional problems, or you simply want to enjoy life at a higher level. It will teach you how to grow beyond old thinking and behaviors, even if those emotional habits are well-established.

The Recovery, Inc. program's strong, positive effects first served as my vehicle to conquer severe panic and depression. The same concepts continue to guide me through *every* new challenge and adventure along the path of life. By using these principles in my daily routine, I have met the demands of returning to school, starting a new profession and relocating to another part of the country. I have an edge—the tools to extinguish anxiety and fear in *any* situation. What began as symptom-management has evolved into life-management.

If you want to improve the quality of your life, this

program offers common sense and logic. The practices are my foundation for emotional well-being. If some methods sound familiar, maybe it is time to incorporate them into your everyday life. As you read, identify with what you learn. Ask yourself, "Where can I apply this?" Then, follow up and do it! Inner peace does not magically wash over you in one day. It is a process. See if any "lights go on." Highlight and reread the sections that strike a note. Please do not expect to scan through the book one time and improve. Study, practice and repetition are the keys to success. Energy and commitment are part of the program. The rewards are lifelong. You can improve *every* aspect of your life!

People often ask why I continue to attend weekly Recovery, Inc. meetings. The answers are simple. As a group leader I am able give back to the program that restored my mental balance and my life. I consider weekly meetings an inexpensive insurance plan. I have regained my mental health, participating in the meetings helps me maintain it. Year after year, my life is better and better. I have grown beyond who I was prior to my illness, and I function at higher levels than ever before.

People often say they wish they could "go back" to a certain time in their life. I don't. I know that <u>today is the best day of my life</u>! I live up to my full potential because I live with inner peace.

My life is better only because I chose to take constructive action to make it better. Once I gained knowledge, I put it into practice. If you expect to change and grow, you have to make the same investment. *True life improvements happen because of your efforts, not someone else's efforts.*

The methods in this book are simple. If you find yourself thinking, "I'm smart, why didn't I think of that?," set aside the self-blame. You are reading this book for what you can gain from it. Be thankful the concepts hit home!

If you tend to resist new ideas, try to be more open-minded. You are in the world to gain knowledge, to grow, to live and enjoy life. Look closely at the ideas you resist. They may have a message for you. Very often we resist changing what needs to be changed the most.

Everyone I know in the program wishes they would have had some solid life-training at an earlier age. If you have picked up this book, you have obviously had similar thoughts. The academic world did not prepare us for the one most vital lesson in life: how to handle our basic emotional responses to the assault of daily irritations and frustrations. "Life school" is where we really grow up—and sometimes fall down.

Because of Recovery, Inc., my world has changed dramatically. I possess the keys to a positive, satisfying existence. I am calm, relaxed and comfortable. I enjoy life. I do not struggle through it, nor am I afraid of it. I discovered that being stressed, depressed, angry and anxious isn't the way life has to be. I have gained improved emotional, physical and spiritual health, self-leadership and confidence in every area of my life—personal, social and professional. Most important of all, I have acquired inner strength from inner peace.

I am sharing the Method I live so that you, too, can enrich your life and attain *Peace of Body and Peace of Mind*.

Author's Note:

This book outlines the phases in my path to mental fitness:

1) The techniques used to overcome incapacitating symptoms and facilitate the transition out of the acute phase.

2) The methods that launched a full healing and allow me to maintain the peace and harmony I enjoy today.

When a specific Recovery, Inc. term or technique is mentioned for the first time, it is highlighted in ***bold-face italic***. In most cases these are not direct quotes from the Recovery, Inc. textbooks, but paraphrased as I learned them at Recovery, Inc. meetings.

Part One

Introduction To Mental Fitness

1. *Who Needs Lessons In Mental Fitness?*

The entire Recovery, Inc. Method revolves around reducing the stress of EVERYDAY life. The time-proven stress-management techniques are a valuable asset to every person who lives, breathes and thinks. Everyone faces nervous tension and all of us need methods to alleviate tension.

By using Recovery,Inc. techniques you gain:

- Freedom from conflicts that keep you in turmoil
- Direction to a free and more peaceful life
- A solid base of self-esteem and confidence
- An understanding of how to change your life for the better
- A calm, rational approach to the many dimensions of your life

It isn't only the traumas of major life events such as accidents, divorce or death that cause an aftermath of stress. Everyday stress builds up and causes the same damage as high-intensity incidents. The demands placed on us in our rapid-paced, ever-changing personal environments bombard us on a regular basis. The effects of everyday stress go unnoticed because they creep in silently.

Our bodies and our minds are suffering. We live in an era when two out of three visits to the family physician are the result of stress-related disorders. Between 50 and 80 percent of the illnesses in the world are considered to be stress-related and psychosomatic in origin. The National Institute of Mental Health (NIMH), estimates that each year in the United States, more than 41 million adults suffer from some form of mental health disorder.

Physical health has always been a value. Through

19

research, education and public awareness we have evolved to taking better care of our bodies. We have the guidelines to follow that enable us to contribute to our physical well-being in a positive way. We are constantly advised about proper nutrition and exercise, what is damaging and what is best for our bodies. When it comes to healthy bodies we are well-informed.

Unfortunately, maintaining good mental health is not a popular notion. We are uneducated when it comes to taking good care of our minds. We shun references to the words "mind" and "mental." We need to be aware that *optimum health is the combination of good mental and physical health.*

Emotional or mental problems have nothing to do with a person's IQ, character or inner strength. As with any other illness, mental illness has no social, ethnic or economic distinctions, and it is age-neutral. I know many highly successful people in the Recovery, Inc. program, business owners and people with multiple university degrees. Well-educated, highly motivated people are not spared emotional problems because of their intelligence. Ph.D.'s or common folks, we are all vulnerable.

I have met people in the health profession—social workers, doctors and nurses—who are shocked to find themselves in the grips of a mental or emotional illness. These professionals don't necessarily feel intellectually above those of us with no medical training. But, many do assume they should be somewhat immune to problems because they have studied and understand mental disorders. These health professionals experience more stigma than the rest of the general population. They come to realize no one truly knows a mental disorder until they have lived it.

Our bodies and minds are not separate entities. Recovery, Inc. taught me to recognize the link, the close union of peace that exists between the two. Physical illness generates anxiety and complications to the emotional part of our humanness and emotional disorders create physical symptoms. Stress is a mind/body affliction. Research shows that stress weakens our immune systems and robs our bodies of physical energy. As our stress levels change, our immune systems respond differently and we are in different states of physical health at different times of our lives. Because stress also robs our minds of emotional strength, we are in different states of mental health at different times of our lives.

Stress causes distress. It causes physical tension and mental tension. It affects our moods, thoughts, bodies and behavior. When you feel tense, you are not living at the top level of your mental fitness.

How does your system respond to tension? What are *your* body and mind symptoms? The number one answer is feeling tired. If you are like most people, you have become used to feeling fatigued. It is so much a part of your life, you take it for granted. Other warning signals of stress include an entire assortment of nagging aches and pains in your head, neck, back and stomach. Stress and strain can make you feel uneasy, on edge, or burned out. You may feel overwhelmed, vulnerable, confused and helpless; angry, sad and out of control. Stress can make you feel as if you just "can't cope."

Stress creates frustrated people. How do you react to stress? Do you become aggressive? Argue? Blow your stack and take out your anger on the people around you? Do you yell at your children as an outlet for your tension? Or do you retreat? Drink alcohol? Cry? Work harder or feel sorry for yourself? Does your tension lead to understress: boredom, or the feeling that your "get up and go" got up and left? Does your little inner critic go into overtime spewing out negative thoughts?

What areas of your life are harmed by stress? Your health, job, relationships? Do you feel that there is nothing in your life that you enjoy. How many *great* days can you count in a single week? Be honest.

Some of us can look back to childhood and recognize having sensitive stress receptors—reacting to circumstances and "feeling" at a different, deeper level. Living with a sensitive stress receptor means being more nervous, upset, humiliated and hurt in situations that don't seem to bother other people. It is common to go through periods when your emotions seem to reside close to the surface. As human beings we are always changing, and it is not unusual to develop a nervous sensitivity later in life.

In Recovery, Inc. I learned that although I was an individual with less resistance to stress, I did not have to condemn myself because of it. Just because you may not have a handle on life pressures right now, does not mean you can't learn to eliminate most of your tension. You CAN build up a resistance to the stress in your everyday life. Not a tolerance, a resistance. There is a huge difference. Tolerance means you can cope. Resistance means that the stress does not affect you. It does not reach your inner being and rattle your inner peace.

When stress overpowers you, it attacks your whole being, your body and your mind. Stress results in digestive or eating disorders, angina, heart attacks, anxiety, depression, panic attacks or any one of hundreds of other serious disturbances which interfere with peaceful living. Stress reduction is symptom reduction. When you exterminate stress, you restore physical energy and emotional strength. Reducing stress is especially important to persons with mental health difficulties. Too much stress can cause a relapse of a condition.

Most stress-lowering techniques encourage us to take time out for ourselves. They aim at helping our bodies fight off the effects of tension that builds up. Many people deal successfully with body stress by exercising. Count the number of health clubs in your local area and the ads for home work-out equipment.

Many inexpensive relaxation techniques work well. Walking, listening to music and meditation calm the body and mind—if you take the time. That is the key—time. When you are overloaded with daily tasks, taking on another does not seem feasible, even when it is beneficial to your mind and body. We have all wished for more hours in the day to accomplish the things we need or want to do.

My all-time favorite, impractical piece of advice for when you are stressed out is to take a hot bath. Now really, how many of us have the luxury of telling our bosses we are leaving work in the middle of the day? Or in the middle of the morning for that matter? A 9:00 a.m. meeting can have you wound up by 10:00 a.m.

Take a few seconds right now to work up a mental total of the stressful hours in your day. Examine your activities: the commute, the job and the hours on the phone; the errands and responsibilities. Then compute the stress time. Pretty high? Now tally your relaxation hours. What is the ratio of your relaxation time to your stress time? Not even close is it? Fifteen minutes a day, or a long weekend every few months, are not going to effectively rid you of stress.

When stress makes us shaky or upset, we need practical skills. Tension needs to be handled throughout the day, not hours later when it has reached colossal proportions. Picture two mounds of dirt. One weighs only a pound, the other a ton. Which takes less time and effort to move? The only way to neutralize the effects of stress, and eliminate the strain from your life is to take clear steps throughout the day. Responding to life's challenges with increased flexibility requires regular practice. Detaching from struggle and frustration does not require detaching from life.

It is likely you have lived with the effects of stress so long that they are invisible to you. Being dissatisfied with life, living with anxious thoughts or low grade depression is not healthy. It is common to blame irritability and feeling "down" on work, school, the weather, parents, partners, children, siblings, the car or the economy. I truly believed that if my world would change, then my problems would disappear. I didn't find out it was me who had to change until a year after I began having panic attacks, quit a job and became virtually housebound. Please—don't wait as long!

Nearly all of us, young or old, have emotional

difficulties at some time in our life. These range from mild to severe. Some of us bounce back when we are thrown off balance by a single event or series of events. Those of us who don't, develop serious problems and long term or intense symptoms. Our suffering lingers and becomes part of life. We live an existence that lacks any hope of relief.

Some people are able to function, work and raise families. But there is no peace or pleasure to their days. Life consists of constant tension. Every day, often every hour, is a battle—a battle of "just getting by." People with nervous problems work hard to keep their affliction quiet and secret. We are experts when it comes to making excuses.

- The excuse, I'm just not hungry; the reality, I am so nervous I don't think I can swallow.
- The excuse, it is less expensive to have my wife cut my hair; the reality, I can't stand to sit still, I feel panicky and confined at the barber shop.
- The excuse, I'm tired or I have to work late; the reality, I can't stand the crowds at my child's little league games.

These excuses don't mean, "I don't want to." They mean, "I can't—I simply can't face the terror, the fear that lives inside me."

I played the game and concealed the depth of what I was experiencing. I longed to do things other people could do, but I simply could not. I couldn't accomplish certain simple feats because of the inner chaos I felt. The first time I faced the reality that I was "just getting by" was when I missed my brother's college graduation. The entire family went to the event, everyone but me. They were there to witness and celebrate. I stayed at home wondering whether I would ever escape my life of hell. I had made the trip when my brother started school at Michigan Tech. A few years later, a 10-hour car trip and a single night at a hotel were totally out of the realm of possibilities. That is when I realized that I wasn't "living," I was just surviving. And I wanted more from life.

Depression or panic can seem to come "out of the blue" and devastate your life. It is not unusual to be fully functioning, then suddenly feel as though your world has crumbled. You may not want to eat or you may overeat. You may have trouble sleeping or sleep too much. It can feel as though an unknown force is controlling your life. It is a terrifying existence because you don't know what to do, or where to turn.

People who suffer from intense physical symptoms make the rounds of medical specialists only to be told there is nothing physically wrong. When you suffer intense body sensations, it is difficult to believe an uncontrollable combination of heart palpitations, headaches, or dizziness; excessive sweating, muscle aches, or nausea; a choking sensation, shortness of breath, or body tremors, could be psychological rather than physiological in nature.

If you feel severely fatigued, isolated, restless, helpless, have difficulty making decisions or have a tape player in your mind spewing out thoughts in fast forward mode, it is often more difficult to identify a treatable problem. Turbulent physical sensations are not there to shock you into awareness.

I have lived my dark night of the soul. I suffered the torture of panic attacks and the deep depression that accompanies them. I avoided all of the places where the panics occurred, and all of the places where I thought they might occur. My world grew smaller and smaller. In the space of two months, I went from being an independent person to being nearly housebound. The clinical label for this disorder is agoraphobia.

I don't know if I had a classic nervous breakdown, although I have used the term to describe what I went through. I do know I was mentally and emotionally unable to cope with life. I was totally overwhelmed and couldn't do anything to help myself.

2. *Where There Is Hope There Can Be Healing*

If you have experienced long-time or severe suffering, I have an important message for you. *"There are NO hopeless cases."* That phrase is one of the most powerful messages in the Recovery, Inc. program. "No hopeless cases." Absolutely none! You do not have to learn to live with what you are going through. A mental health challenge does not mean the life you once knew is over.

Prior to joining Recovery, Inc., none of the professionals I had contact with, none of the books I read, had even touched on the theme, *"There are NO hopeless cases."* Dr. Abraham Low, Recovery, Inc.'s founder, believed it with all his heart, and worked diligently to transfer the conviction to his patients. He repeatedly told them they would become well. I know the deep meaning of hopeless and powerless. I know how it feels to be lost and dejected. I know despair. During my illness, I had no expectation of a "normal" life. There was a time when I viewed death as a comfortable alternative to my suffering.

Recovery, Inc. furnishes the keys for self in-powerment and mental fitness. It equips you with the means to expel the sense of helplessness. It replaces helplessness with hope and the pride of accomplishment.

The short but powerful message, "No hopeless cases," supplied my first spark of hope. The feeling of hope wavered more times than I can count. Whenever grave doubts returned and threatened my progress, I repeated the phrase, "There are no hopeless cases." The simple statement was the catalyst that fueled my will to live and grow. It was there when I needed it most. My spark of hope kindled into a flame. Today I hold the statement as a truth, not an opinion. There are no hopeless cases! I know it with every fiber of my being.

How can I believe with such certainty? Over the years in Recovery, Inc., I have met several people who have been diagnosed with schizophrenia, bi-polar (manic-depressive) disorder, agoraphobia, borderline personality disorder. Others have struggled with clinical depression, panic disorder, obsessive-compulsive disorder, seasonal affective disorder (SAD), combat and sexual abuse related post traumatic stress disorder (PTSD) and eating disorders - people with dual disorders, (addiction plus emotional or psychiatric illnesses), individuals who have attempted suicide, had shock treatments or were back-ward patients. Everyone thought their own particular difficulty was insurmountable. Today these people are healthy, functioning members of society. They are the rule, not the exception, for those who take self-management seriously. Today they are living, not just existing.

They are living, breathing proof that mental health can be improved. Some individuals were told by the "system" that they would never become well, that they would never again be able to work, or to live by themselves. They proved the system wrong. They are productive, and no longer depend on social security disability income.
Recovery, Inc. provides more than hope. Recovery, Inc. furnishes specific techniques that remove the restrictions of debilitating mental and physical distress. It provides the vehicle to reduce the stresses of everyday life. Reduce stress and you reduce the risk of relapse.

Remember, there are no hopeless cases. That includes YOU. Every one of you.

3. *Why Me?*

If we do not like where we are, who we are, or how we feel, part of the wellness process is to look for the "why." If we know the causes, we attempt to avoid or correct them. We certainly try to steer clear of them in the future. We do not want to continue on an unhealthy path.

The fact is that you behave and react the way you do because of everything you learned in the past. Whether it was conscious learning or reactive learning—you are who you are, on this day, at this moment, because you live your reality and become a product of it.

The adult child of an alcoholic who has problems can point to a childhood filled with constant or intermittent chaos. A parent may have been physically or mentally abusive. The outcome is resentment toward the alcoholic parent and lack of respect for the spouse that chose to stay in the relationship, and expose the child(ren) to the lifestyle. For anyone who suffered abuse or witnessed it, there are distinct reasons for why they feel, what they feel.

It is much different for those of us who grew up in stable homes. Why did we turn out the way we did? Why was I over-sensitive to negative comments? What made me think I wasn't as good as my older sister? Even as an adult I tried to prove I was a good daughter. What made me believe I wasn't as worthy as everyone else? What made the perfectionist in me blossom? Why did I always seek the approval of others? What gave me a fine-tuned excessive sense of responsibility? Why did I feel alone, even when I wasn't? What accounted for my lack of self-esteem that went back to early childhood? Genetic susceptibility? Birth order? Karma? The questions can be never-ending when there is no clear-cut, striking reason for your mental state.

I did not come from a classic dysfunctional family. I had no one to fault but myself for my warped thoughts. As most other people, I can identify a few points which contributed to the "why" of who I was. The following statements are made without *any* blame. I passed through my fault-finding stage many years ago.

In the 40 plus years they were married, I rarely heard my parents discuss, much less argue about anything. It was their choice of behavior. Millions of people grow up in the same kind of placid atmosphere (which is far better than an aggressive one). But it is difficult to learn the art of self-expression if you have never been exposed to it. Although I value the formal education I received, the private school I attended for twelve years was the kind where you did what you were told—period. We were there to learn and behave. Or maybe it was to behave and learn. The atmosphere contributed to acting or not acting out of fear. My religious instruction emphasized gloom, doom and sin. It indoctrinated not only the feeling of not being good enough, but also the idea that I never could be. This segment of my upbringing fostered more fear.

In the process of identifying the "why," I learned an important truth: The "why" uncovered the past. It did not change present thinking or behavior. I was still depressed and panicky. This book is not about the "why." It will not help you delve into your past or understand the subconscious reasons behind your difficulty. It will teach you "HOW" to deal with life's issues, the everyday stresses that build on each other and sometimes immobilize you.

Most of us want to know the reason "why" because we never want to repeat the same distress and torture. The investigative phase is natural and healthy. Everyone I know who has had problems has gone through a stage of questioning "what" and "why." Unfortunately, many of us become caught up in the "why." Being obsessed with the "why" isn't healthy. Constant focus on the "why" prolongs the wellness process. Ask yourself if you are gaining ground by exploring the past and living in regret. Some of us will never know the real "why." Accept it and move forward.

Whatever the trigger or cause, childhood trauma, or adult life event, your situation is not unique. If you insist that your underlying reasons are different, you are limiting your ability to move ahead. Millions of other people feel the same doubts, fears, and anxieties. Whatever the origin, you have carried learned behavior into your life, and you operate within the guidelines of that learned behavior. You do, however, have choices. You can correct the behavior or you can keep analyzing it. You can't beat the "*why*" to death. It exists. It will not go away. NOW is what you can work on. You will not totally forget your past, but you can stop actively bringing it to the forefront of your mind.

I learned that when I concentrated on "why," I was stealing precious energy I could be using for the "how" to improve my health. I finally realized I was using up my present life by dwelling on and digging into the past. I took the mental energy I was putting into the why, and channelled it into the NOW. I had to make a conscious decision. Perhaps you do, too. Try these next statements on for size. "From this moment, I will concentrate on my recovery and not the cause. I accept who I am and move forward with conviction."

Life's most important lessons are learned when you are "growing out" of difficult situations, not while you are "going through" them.

Knowing even some of the WHY you are WHO you are, does not erase the negative thoughts you have today. Your past exists as part of your present world. Another fact is: you *can* change. Picture yourself making a U-turn to change your direction from past to future. From then to now. It is your choice. You can be less judgmental of yourself and others. You can change what you think, how you react and how you feel. You can be more calm, more assertive. You can be your own best friend and learn to like yourself. You can change YOU. You can be the person you have always wanted to be.

4. *Blame Versus Responsibility*

Taking responsibility for yourself and your life does not include feeling guilty about who or where you are today. Taking responsibility for wellness is very different than taking the blame for illness. Taking responsibility for your wellness in the present, allows room for growth. Blaming yourself for the past holds you hostage. You are who you are, whatever the state of your present emotional condition. You cannot change the facts of how you became who you are today. But you can shape your future, from this moment forward.

A few years ago, because of my interest in mental health, I attended a friends and family seminar at a Veteran's Administration Hospital. A portion of the day was spent at a group session with 20 Vietnam Veterans who were at the tail end of a 28-day program for Post Traumatic Stress Disorder (PTSD). During the discussion, several veterans made reference to the fact that they had made the choice to enlist, rather than wait to be drafted. Their stories reflected regret, anguish and self-blame. It was clear that they believed their lives would have turned out different had they not enlisted. Perhaps they would not be in that hospital, in that treatment program, in that room, telling their story. It was obvious that they were entrenched in the idea that they had made a wrong decision. Their lives would have been much better, much better, "If only ... "

A few weeks later I discussed my concern about the veterans' strong self-blame with a friend who had been in the same PTSD program. I asked him if he blamed himself for his decision to join the service. He replied, with no hesitation, "Of course, I have to take responsibility." Part of these Vietnam Veterans' fixed belief system, their programming, is holding them accountable for a decision they made more than 25 years ago. I don't know if that is what they are told, or if it is their interpretation. I do know, however, that there is more than one person in that group who thinks the same way.

The true meaning of responsibility means taking care of yourself now, in the present—today! Continuing to condemn yourself for a past act, a past decision, keeps you trapped in the past. In order to create a new life, you must stop clinging to the past.

How many other people, with other difficulties, are doing the same thing—marching in place instead of moving forward? Are you holding on to anything in your past that you consider to be a mistake? Something in which you had a choice? Do you dwell on it every once in a while, or often? Is it a marriage? A divorce? Your choice of colleges? A job decision? A move? These not-so-wise decisions contributed to who you are today. But so did other circumstances. Good, bad, and indifferent.

If you are rooted in self-blame because of a past decision, you can choose to stay inside those barriers, or choose to use the same energy and same strong conviction to move forward. You can re-channel the responsibility for what *did* happen, to what *can* happen.

Popular theory used to shove the blame for psychological problems on a person's parents or upbringing. According to one of today's theories, that blame has shifted to the victim, the patient. Do healers believe for one minute that a patient in the midst of an illness can benefit from the suggestion that he or she caused their condition? People who face mental health challenges feel worthless. They do not need outside influences reinforcing that sense of worthlessness.

Illness is rarely caused by a single factor. You can point to the fat content of foods as one of the causes of cancer or heart disease. But, other factors contribute as well. What do you point to when there is an emotional problem? Do you blame it on the fact that you ingested lead by chewing on your crib rail when you were 10 months old?

When I was sick I buried myself under a ton of self-induced guilt. No one had to plant the idea of self-blame in my head. Thank God, no "authority" told me it was "my fault" I began having panic attacks. I probably would have considered myself evil. The accusation would have been another blow to my already fragile mental state. People with health problems feel scared and confused. They need to be guided out of confusion, not led into more of it.

This is how I interpret a statement which suggests I originated my sickness: "Shame on you Rose, you have turned yourself into a mental case." My opinion, my translation. You might think it is strong. It may not be my first response, but I would reach that conclusion sooner or later. If this is how I see it, there are other people who would perceive the concept in the same way, as an accusation. When a doctor casts the shadow of blame on the patient, no matter how many positive statements come out of that professional's mouth, that shadow of one statement will do enormous damage to the person's mind, body and soul. It opens a new wound. A wound that will fester before it heals.

Faulting someone for a condition is not a motivation tool. People can be encouraged to become self-directed, active participants in their wellness process without blaming themselves for their condition. Is telling someone they are to blame a positive thought? Does it instill hope? Does it help a person move ahead towards wellness, or, does it focus on what might have been?

To me, the theory of self-inflicted illness is more destructive than constructive. It is as detrimental as the erroneous belief that mental disorder is a punishment from God. It is as negative as a minister who tells parents that their child's illness (physical or emotional) is the result of their sins—another "authority" figure laying blame. When a human being is sick we need to drop, "who needs to be accountable" and move ahead to the healing process.

I learned a long time ago my illness was *"Fate" appointed*. I have never heard or read anything else by Dr. Low which explains the statement much further. He kept ideas simple. My translation of "Fate appointed illness" is: The condition is real. It is mine. I did not request it. I have

no one to blame. I do not have to feel guilty.
This is my truth. It is a healthy truth.

Part Two

Facts For Mental Fitness

5. *Common Threads*

Disorders have many common threads or symptoms. Let me illustrate. Picture an assortment of fabric pillows with colored stripes running left to right on a white background. Each single color represents a particular characteristic, feeling, sensation or behavior pattern. Each pillow has a label corresponding to each separate diagnosis listed in DSM-IV (Diagnostic and Statistical Manual) the professional's diagnostic bible: clinical depression, agoraphobia, self-defeating personality disorder.

Imagine blue threads represent lack of self-esteem. Red threads signify sleeplessness, green threads symbolize anxiety and yellow, restlessness. Other colors correspond to: fatigue, irritability, pessimism, burnout; fear of change and fear of social situations; agitation, confusion, isolation; internalizing feelings; being uncomfortable when alone or in a crowd.

Each and every pillow in the assortment would be laced with the same colors. Only the width of a particular color would be different. Most of the fabric would have several strands of blue, which represent lack of self-esteem. Different diagnosed conditions have different proportions of many characteristics. Persons with anxiety disorder experience depression. Individuals with any degree of depression are irritable, so are those with PTSD. Many diagnoses include some kind of sleep irregularity. Isolation is also common.

Being human means having feelings, sensations, thoughts and impulses. These can be calm and pleasant, or distressing and unpleasant. Experts tell us that there must be a significant level of distress or impairment in order to classify illness as a disorder. I suspect the designation is rather simple in some illnesses, but not everyone fits neatly into a precise diagnosis. Mental health problems are not as easily catalogued as library books.

You may question how a single method is used to overcome such a vast variety of problems. The answer is simple. This mental fitness system targets symptoms: feelings, sensations, thoughts and impulses. Symptoms are the commonality. Recovery, Inc.'s techniques are beneficial with or without a label. This isn't only my interpretation. Dr. Low's Method teaches you how to eliminate symptoms, develop habits to enrich mental health, and remove self-imposed limits. Why delay improving your mental fitness until you qualify for a label from the psychiatric community?

You will not find many diagnostic labels in Dr. Low's textbooks. The genius doctor had passed on long before I began attending meetings, so I don't know his exact reasoning. I suspect he did not want to burden people with frightening clinical designations that set limits. He was very careful with his choice of words. Nothing points to any condition being hopeless.

He does use one generic expression throughout his writings, the term *nervous patient*. Although it is a harmless label, I had some trouble with it at first because of my sensitive nature. I did not want to accept the fact that I had a mental problem. What helped change my attitude were the other members of the group. I was in awe of many of them when I learned how much their lives had improved. They did not take offense to the term. They were comfortable referring to themselves as nervous patients. As I looked around I found that I was more well than some, less well than others. I certainly did have problems with "nerves." *Webster's II* defines a "patient" as one who suffers. I qualified. It wasn't long before I felt comfortable calling myself a "nervous patient." After all, it is just an expression. Today, some people prefer the words mental health consumer or mental health survivor. Times change, expressions change.

What you find in Dr. Low's works are descriptive passages about numerous diverse symptoms. There are references to simple anxiety, crying spells, anger and neurotic behavior. There are narratives on the perfectionist and the worry wart. Professionals, and those of us who are well-read, can identify post-partum depression, manic-depressive illness, obsessive-compulsive disorder and a host of other phobias and illnesses from the patient interviews depicted throughout the pages. I connected with the topics because Dr. Low's writings describe what people think and how they feel. As I read I thought, "Yes, that's me! I've felt that way!"

Emotional and nervous problems are universal. Unfortunately we are not encouraged or instructed to seek possible solutions before difficulties grow to significant levels or critical proportions. If our awareness ran parallel to our problems, it would certainly save an enormous amount of personal misery. This book was written with two audiences in mind: those of you who have suffered from a diagnosed emotional, nervous or mental problem, and the millions of you who have no label, but live with some degree of nervousness or in some degree of personal pain. We all need resources. If you do not believe it, ask yourself why this book is in your hands right now. Everything in life happens for a reason.

If I was asked to identify a single leading character trait common to everyone in the program, I would say it is perfectionism. Being a perfectionist means you strive to be THE BEST at EVERYTHING. It means you feel wrong when the outcome is not absolutely right. Because perfectionism does not allow for mistakes, you live in constant frustration. Very little reaches your expectations, which causes you to be disappointed with yourself and with life in general.

I believe whatever the outward manifestations, the root of ALL emotional problems is lack of self-esteem. Some call it self-worth, others call it self-confidence. Many factors contribute to the feeling (or lack of it). We compare ourselves to society's standards or to our own. The bottom line is that, in our own minds, we don't measure up. We feel deficient and different.

Feelings, sensations and symptoms are the same for

each of us. It is only the degree of intensity and frequency that differs. I have experienced various levels of nervousness. I have worked on a single difficulty and several at a time. I first worked on the severe problems then, the less severe. Believe me, it took a long time for the apprehension of public speaking to make it to the top of my list. Simple tasks—driving, shopping, eating in public, interacting with people—were skills I had to re-learn. Once I re-established the basics, I chose to meet other challenges in other areas. I chose to grow.

In his book, *The Sky's the Limit*, Dr. Wayne Dyer talks about how modern medicine (psychology included) focuses on the elimination of symptoms instead of on a more growth-oriented approach. There is scant attention in the mind area of "medicine" which focuses beyond coping. We are not encouraged to cultivate habits to enrich our mental health.

Every aspect of the Recovery, Inc. program guides us to develop healthy habits and to grow beyond self-limiting patterns. Through its teachings and my efforts in implementing those teachings, I have become one of the "no-limit people" Wayne Dyer writes about. Because of my Recovery training, I keep challenging myself and continue to grow.

About three years into my practice of Recovery, Inc. principles, I was quite satisfied with who I had become. I was better than my old self, and my life was acceptable. As I continued to practice, my life continued to improve. Today my life is great! I have gone from being immobilized in mind and body, to speaking in front of large audiences and appearing on radio and TV shows. My situation is not unique. There are many, many more individuals such as me. For more than half a century Recovery, Inc. has been teaching people to remove their self-imposed limits.

6. *Myths Surrounding Self-Help*

Misunderstanding and myths—because of them we forego experiences, knowledge and growth. How many times have you finally decided to try something, found out it worked for you in your life, and said: "I wish I would have done this years ago?"

My Dad was a staunch believer in staying on the ground. He was 72 years old before he took his first airplane trip. Once he discovered flying, there was no holding him back. During the next five years he traveled to more states than ever before. Once he conquered his apprehension, air-travel provided him a vast new world of experiences.

The term, "Self-help," is often misunderstood. For many people the word self-help conjures up a collection of dreadful ideas. Do you realize that your individual growth is the result of an entire series of individual improvements? Look at the meaning of the words:

Individual = self   Improvements = help

You possess certain skills today because you acquired information and applied that information. You have been self-helping all your life. Stop and think about it. Someone showed you how to feed yourself with a spoon. You practiced the movement over and over, and eventually learned how to transfer food from a bowl, into your mouth. Until you perfected your aim, you wore a lot of the food you wanted to eat. Slowly, the act of eating changed from a challenge to a skill.

Other life skills you take for granted now, talking, dressing, writing, riding a bike, driving a car, were learned the same way. Each skill required instruction from people or books, and practical application on your part. Sometimes you were alone when you received instructions and information, sometimes you were in a group. Self-help information is how-to information.

As an adult you continue to learn through self-help information. How? Through business seminars, do-it-yourself classes, motivational courses, financial planning sessions, spirituality workshops and every non-fiction book you read. Changing spark plugs or cake decorating, mastering a software program or golf, learning Spanish or hot air-ballooning—it is all self-help. It comes in all shapes, sizes and mediums: a semester of classes, one-day seminars, videos, audio-tapes, books and magazine articles. The motivating factor can be financial gain or self-improvement. Occasionally you master a skill simply because you are interested in a subject. In other cases it is required. You may want to take a yoga class, but your job or degree require more academic subjects.

Learning is not just for children. If you truly want to grow beyond who you are today, in any area of your life, you must be able to say, "I am *willing* to learn."

Too many people shy away from "traditional" self-help and support because they do not know what it entails. Those of you who have never attended a session, may think it involves a group of people disclosing all that ails them. Ninety-nine percent of the time, that couldn't be further from the truth. Group support was developed as a means of communicating information to more than a single individual during a single time frame. As in academic classes, the material is presented to more than one person at a time.

Support groups are groups that encourage and enlighten individuals with common interests, difficulties or predicaments. People attend meetings because there is consolation in knowing others are surviving the same life lessons. When you attend group sessions, you discover that you are not unique in what you feel and think.

The best support groups are those which encourage an individual to be *self-directed*. They promote hope, acceptance, and health.

There are a small percentage of groups that label themselves "support," when in fact they are simply a place where people meet to complain about life. This type group serves no purpose, except to foster and reinforce self-pity. The steady diet of moaning and groaning crystallizes the beliefs of "poor me" and magnifies "I can't."

There are no goals for self-improvement. Participants are content trading war stories. There is a subtle form of competition as to who is "most miserable." Some persons enjoy this type of group because they like to complain. Perhaps it is all they know. Once a week or once a month they have a ready and willing audience.

If you find yourself leaving an open-forum support meeting, time after time, feeling as bad or worse than when you walked in, think about the focus. Was the central theme dysfunction and disability or wellness and ability?

Self-help is a step beyond support. The core objectives are education plus genuine support. A self-help group is a source of information, a place where you learn the how to's of self-improvement. Self-help meetings are a place to gain knowledge. The "self" part of the equation means *you* take the knowledge and use it. The "help" part of the equation includes life skills, motivation, guidance and encouragement.

Many of us were brought up to think we "should" be able to "do it on our own." We do try, and when we fail, we think it is because we are not smart enough or sturdy enough. We feel lost and afraid. Not having all the answers does not mean we are illiterate, dumb or stupid. In truth, no one on earth has all the answers. Reaching out for direction, does not mean we are defective or deficient. It is tough to admit something isn't quite right. Any first step is difficult, but, the sooner you take it, the faster you will be able to handle daily life with strength, dignity and inner calm.

When you encounter a mental health challenge, it is typical to wonder if you are beyond being able to help yourself. If you are confused about who you are and where your life is going, you may even question whether you will be able to retain any details because of your present state of mind. You absorb ideas and life principles by listening. If your ears can hear, you will learn. If your eyes can read, you will learn. You *are* capable of learning and acting on new knowledge, no matter what your present state of life. Self-help supplies information on "how" to move forward. You do not have to be able to pay strict attention.

People fear self-help meetings because they think they will be required to reveal everything about themselves. The reality is, you do not have to share your past. What you want to keep private, you can keep private. It is not at all like psychotherapy. You will listen more than you speak.

Self-help promotes growth. You learn to be active, not passive, in dealing with life. Self-help initiates positive changes—changes that can alter the course of your life for the better. All of us want a better life. Self-help is for people who are open-minded, open to growing. It may not be for everyone. You will never know unless you experience it first hand.

Recovery, Inc.'s self-help and support supplies solid, structured direction. It may be unique, in that most of the instruction comes in the form of examples—examples from real people, with real challenges, and real solutions. Through the examples, you learn when and how to use basic life skills. You hear how others use the principles in their everyday lives to reduce tension and stress in a natural way. You witness practical application and authentic results. You learn *exactly* what other individuals are doing to cross the bridge to a fuller life.

People are probably most apprehensive about attending a self-help group which deals with mental health issues because they "don't want to sit around with a bunch of sick people." If you have this picture in your mind, you might be as surprised as I was when I attended my first self-help meeting. The group members appeared and acted so well, so "together," so healthy, I doubted whether any of their conditions had been as severe as mine. Self-help is not only for the "down and out." People who attend are at all stages of wellness. Recovery, Inc. meetings concentrate on wellness, not illness. It is a mental *health* group, not a mental illness group.

7. *Trusting And Accepting The System*

It is typical to doubt any program when you don't understand all the aspects and when everything else you have tried hasn't had any long-standing positive effects. I embraced and trusted Recovery, Inc.'s lessons because both the founder and the program possess excellent credentials.

By the time I joined the organization, people had been using Dr. Low's Method for mending minds for forty-four years. Common sense told me that an organization and a mental health system which had survived more than four decades, was solid and stable.

This system of healthy mind techniques was developed, tested and refined over years of working with in-patients, research patients and private practice patients. In addition to his practice in psychiatry and neurology, Dr. Low published papers on group psychotherapy, shock treatment, and lab investigations on mental diseases. He was an authority on mental health and devoted his life to engineering and perfecting this formula of self-help. His aim was for his patients to learn to help themselves. His Method provides people with both the understanding of what generates their symptoms and uncomplicated basic skills to eliminate those symptoms.

Group leaders of Recovery, Inc. are volunteer, peer facilitators. They are individuals who have suffered some type of psychological difficulty, have benefitted from the program and choose to give back to it. Although leaders are required to attend training sessions and are authorized yearly by Recovery, Inc.'s Board of Directors, they are not set apart from the group. They are a part of it. Their reasons for attending are the same as the other members: to stay on the road to wellness.

Recovery, Inc. recognizes that certain aspects of mental health are out of the realm of self-help. The program takes no position on the use of medication, and does not encourage or discourage its use. Drugs and other forms of therapy are not discussed at meetings. Judging the advantages or disadvantages of other forms of treatment is not part of this self-help system. When questions arise, members are directed to check with their professionals.

In addition to the credibility aspect, the Recovery, Inc. system contains common sense philosophies. Anyone can learn to incorporate the approach into daily life. None of Recovery, Inc.'s philosophies are revolutionary. None of the ideas oppose any life values I learned as a child or an adult. In fact, they enhanced them.

From the beginning, I looked forward to attending weekly self-help meetings. You notice I didn't say I was comfortable. It is unlikely that a person with nervous problems would feel completely at ease. I did experience a sense of relief when I found out that I wasn't peculiar, strange or weird because I suffered a mental problem. I wasn't crazy!

There is something magical and comforting about talking face to face with people who have conquered the same feelings you fight daily. Hearing the voice of experience conveys a powerful message of hope and the prospect for healing. I learned that my fears, symptoms, sensations, thoughts and feelings were *average* for a nervous patient. Not average in the sense that the world population experiences them to the same degree, but typical, common and ordinary for a person with a more sensitive stress receptor. When you realize that nervous symptoms, physical manifestations and thoughts are average, you take the first step in removing the fear of the symptoms.

The opposite of average is unique. Unique is defined as "the only one of its kind." Therefore, "average" means it has happened to at least one other person. Very few, if any, circumstances in life are truly unique. And, knowing there were Recovery, Inc. meetings all across the United States, Canada, Ireland and a few other foreign countries was absolute proof that I wasn't the only one in the world who felt alone, afraid, angry and confused.

The emotional climate of a Recovery, Inc. group is an element I still appreciate. There is a certain fellowship, a sense of mutual understanding and acceptance. People can relate to each other's uneasiness and apprehensions. No one thought it strange when I described being so nervous that I had trouble signing my name because my hand trembled. Or that I sometimes feel so confused and nervous that I became disoriented. I know exactly what someone means when they describe feeling tired but edgy, exhausted and nervous at the same time; how it feels to shake from the inside out. I know how you can be afraid to be alone, and at the same time be afraid to be with people. At a group meeting, people see you as a complete person in spite of your difficulties.

Instead of multiplying horror and pain, there is a comforting spirit, an energy created by people in the process of growing. I can honestly say, I have always left a Recovery, Inc. meeting feeling better than when I walked in the door. Even today, I acquire a healthy dose of inspiring stories of progress at every meeting.

Through the program I was able to find individuals I could admire and respect. Although the program does not match up newcomers with formal sponsors, I found role models I tried to emulate, and mentors who helped my progress. It was important to me that I was allowed to make those choices myself. I did not have someone else watching me, I was the monitor. I made progress for me, not to please someone else.

I am the person ultimately in charge of my mental health. I am the one person in charge of my life. I am the full partner in my growth.

At first I envied the Recovery, Inc. people who had support people from outside the program. Husbands, wives, siblings, friends, a loyal "buddy" or buddies they could depend on to make them feel comfortable when they ventured from home. Having another person around adds a sense of safety because they can "take over" if a catastrophe arises. Some companions give willingly, some grudgingly, some are paid. There are people who run million-dollar businesses, and create elaborate networks to stay comfortable. Nevertheless, deep in their hearts, they know they are just "getting by."

If you have a well-established personal support team, you may truly want to become well, but have trouble taking the first step out of your comfort zone. People use all sorts of motivating factors, long-range goals, to help escape their personal traps: I want to finish school and obtain my degree; Someday I want to have a child; I want to walk my daughter up the aisle when she gets married; I want to teach again; I want to be able to take my grandson to a ball game by myself. Some reasons are more compelling: I need to be well enough to work and support my family; My husband is having another affair and I have to get well so I can free myself from this marriage.

Your dreams may be simple. You may want to go to the mall or grocery store unaccompanied. You may want to share dinner with friends at a restaurant. Whatever your ambitions, they are worthy and important.

All the goals have the same underlying message: "I want to be free." If you need a push, a goal, ambition or dream, you will have to pick your own.

If you rely on someone else to prop you up—be honest—you are not genuinely comfortable, because deep inside you are not at peace. You are still confined. In reality, "needing" someone else to trail along with you is ripping away your self-respect, little by little. Even if you work hard at not showing it on the outside, it is taking its toll, as it did with me.

Ask yourself if you are holding hostages to prove to yourself that someone does in fact love or like you. And know that you can love and be loved without need and dependence.

You can learn authentic comfort and be proud of yourself when you accomplish your goals by yourself. Unfortunately you can't just want results, you must work for them. Make your actions match your words. Change, "I want to get well," to "I WILL get well." Modify one word and add conviction to your desire. You can have the greatest cheering squad in the world, but you still have to make yourself move out into the world, as everyone else does.

Some people claim personal family support is a must. I disagree. You may become more self-reliant if you don't have a relative or close friend who is supportive. There was no one special standing by my side. Now I realize that being on my own made me stronger and I am thankful. Because I had no one to lean on, I was more determined to become self-sufficient again. I couldn't be complacent. Interaction with my Recovery, Inc. "family" provided strength, true understanding and continuous support. They believed in my abilities, not my disabilities.

8. *A Framework For Wellness*

A Recovery, Inc. self-help meeting was designed with a framework for optimum learning. The meeting is organized into four distinct sections and each has its own time guidelines.

The first segment consists of reading a chapter from one of Dr. Low's books, or listening to one of his taped lectures. If it is the printed material (and it usually is), each person in the group reads a paragraph or two. If someone doesn't want to participate they can "pass."

The second segment is a focused learning environment of practical, rather than theoretical instruction. It is a time when members share examples about *how* they have used *what* they have learned in the program. It is a time for understandable samples of life-training.

Examples provide answers to basic inquiries such as:

- "How can I feel less stressed and nervous?"
- "I know I have to do something for my depression, but what?"
- "How do I control my angry feelings?"
- "What can I do to reduce this anxiety and stress?"
- "I know I am driving myself crazy about this, but how do I stop?"
- "What can I do to stop my panic attacks?"
- "What do I change and how?"

These real-life accounts demonstrate the sound principles of mental health that lead to inner peace. They are the Recovery, Inc. Method in Action.

Examples are related according to a simple four step format.

Step One: A member describes concise details: the place, time, who or what else may have been involved, and what occurred to provoke the distress. This not only helps paint a picture for others to see, but also sets the tone to be more objective. It presents facts minus emotionalism.

Step Two: The person explains what symptoms he experienced: what he was feeling and thinking.

Step Three: The person tells which Recovery, Inc. techniques were used to calm down and feel more comfortable: how he was able to overcome tension; how he was able to solve what appeared to be a problem.

Step Four: The person reports how he would have reacted in the same or a similar situation before he learned Recovery, Inc. life tools.

This four step format serves many purposes. In addition to providing guidelines as to what to report, it helps expedite the procedure. The outline helped me learn to relate an incident, rather than talk on and on (report instead of complain). It also helps individuals who are unsure of what to say, to illustrate a specific event in some semblance of order.

This "order" was very important to me. When I came into the program everything in my life felt out of order. My framework had collapsed. There was no structure or harmony to my days, or my life. I was floundering. It was a blessing to have some disciplined direction. It added a sense of balance to the disorganization that had taken over my body and mind.

The number of examples during a single meeting depends on the number of people attending, but is rarely more than five. The subjects covered in the examples are events that happen at work, school, home, church, in a hardware store, the car, during business meetings or social events, while watching TV, ironing, working out, talking on the phone. The event can happen during any one of the 1440 minutes of the day: morning, noon or night. It may be "as soon as I woke up," or "while I was eating lunch." It could happen, "on the way to...," or "when I was trying to fall asleep..." The event can involve other people: parents, spouses, children, siblings, bosses, co-workers, or the auto repair person—or no-one else. Nervous symptoms can materialize whether you are in a crowd or alone. Events can happen virtually anywhere, anytime, with anyone.

After one member gives an example, other group members comment on it. We do not evaluate or critique a person's performance. Remarks are directed to the entire group, not only to the person who shares the example. There is no personal or prescriptive phrasing such as: "My reaction was...," or, "You should...," or "Don't..." These guidelines for the comments provide for a simple transfer of information. They safeguard the person who shared the example from feeling criticized or judged. When members comment on an example, they tell what they spotted or saw in the event. Their observations center on enhancing wellness. Comments are stated in Recovery, Inc. terminology for two reasons. It helps keep everyone on the same "wave-length." It also maintains the focus on what is taught within the scope of the program. Dr. Low referred to the Recovery, Inc. techniques as *"spotting" phrases*.

"Spot" means to see, notice or discover. When you look for a friend in a crowd and finally see him, you have "spotted" him despite the swarm of other people. Now take that same meaning and apply it when you are uncomfortable. When you're upset, your mind is swarming with thoughts. Recovery, Inc. techniques are designed to help "spot" or zero in on what you are thinking and to alter those thoughts. The simple phrases, the individual pieces of wisdom, when taken as a whole, are referred to as the Recovery, Inc. Method.

The Method is:

* A training and guidance system that teaches you how to identify and transform confused, faulty thinking, to sound thinking; alter harmful attitudes; change unhealthy actions into beneficial behavior.

* A blueprint of purposeful, powerful, healthy, positive, secure thinking for life training.

* A complete strategy of non-judgmental, self-evaluation tools for better living.

Recovery, Inc. "spotting" phrases or techniques are a useful type of feedback mechanism. They are not meant to grade. They add clarity to WHAT we think and HOW we act. When spotting phrases are used by an individual during personal day-to-day practice, they are a means of self-evaluation. When expressed in group, they are resources and learning tools for both the person who shares an example and the other participants. They remind everyone to set the course for healthier thinking. You will see the special meaning of the "spotting techniques" throughout this book.

If a member has difficulty and can't seem to shake what he or she is feeling, comments from the group supply insight. In addition to specific Recovery, Inc. tools to help relieve inner unrest, comments include some mention of improvement from pre-Recovery, Inc. days. This is often progress that the person who presented the example hasn't been able to recognize. Additional "spotting" brings out more insight to the success aspect of how someone handled a given situation, and it is another way for everyone in the group to learn the Recovery, Inc. spotting techniques.

The program does not target specific relationships: personal, social or work/business. There are no separate male/female issues. These principles work in all areas, in any kind of relationship. They are people principles, life principles. Since the Method covers the gamut of human nervous conditions, you can tailor your individual program to where you are in life. If Recovery's principles can affect change in persons with significant difficulties, think of what they can do for you.

Recovery, Inc. "tools" are transferable to any life situation. They have helped me dispel anxious feelings in tunnels, elevators, and low-ceiling parking structures, on bridges, in trains and planes; when speaking to a single person, to groups of potential customers at trade shows and to gatherings of 200 or more people. They help in every facet of my life. I grow, and my support system—my method for handling life—remains the same. Recovery, Inc. tools—tools for life management.

Examples shared at the meetings are true life experiences. Sometimes they involve circumstances which are not in the general scheme of your personal life. I remember a man in my first group who always gave examples about his experiences in night school. I paid attention and participated, but wasn't really interested. Going to school was not in the realm of possibilities for me at that point of my life. Guess what? A few years later I was well enough to attend classes. It was my turn to face nervousness when it came to professors, lessons, exams and on-campus parking. The examples that man gave about when and how he used his Recovery, Inc. skills to cope with hectic days and restless nights, suddenly became invaluable to me. His experiences benefitted me.

I think of examples as the "listen and learn" part of the meeting. They demonstrate the "how to" in simple, straightforward terms: this is what was happening, and this is what I did to make it stop. Each example describes an instance of strong or mild inner turmoil—an event that robbed the person's inner peace. This is what sets Recovery, Inc. apart from other support programs. The difficulties are described, but so are the solutions.

The third portion of the meeting is devoted to additional comments on examples that were shared, and questions from newcomers.

The fourth and last part of the meeting, "mutual aid," has a more casual atmosphere. It is a time when people can interact one on one, or in smaller circles. As with all other segments of the meeting, participation is encouraged, not required. Some people choose not to speak at all, it is their choice. No one is pressured. During mutual aid a person who is apprehensive about speaking in front of the group may share a problem with one person and gain some insight. An experienced member may be able to suggest some Recovery, Inc. techniques or material in one of the texts that addresses a particular difficulty. "Veterans" often offer information about what circumstances brought them to Recovery, Inc. and how they have improved.

These small conversations lend encouragement to persons who may view their particular illness as unique or hopeless. Speaking with someone who has learned to manage life in a serene manner, is worth more than any statistics and survey results printed in black and white.

For me, participating in mutual aid was a first attempt at functioning in a somewhat social situation. It is where I began to re-learn the art of talking to and making eye contact with people I didn't know well. It was a safe place to start.

The "aid" which is offered and shared during mutual aid is truly reciprocal. Participants who furnish the support are reminded of their own progress. Recipients are reassured that their particular case is not hopeless, that there is every reason to believe that they, too, can improve. The support which is exchanged is convincing because it comes from the heart of a kindred spirit. Mutual Aid in Recovery, Inc. is a time of encouragement, gratitude and hopefulness.

9. *Thoughts—The Power Of Life*

There was a time when I believed just about everything I thought. I assumed that thoughts were an output of the brain. Other body organs work automatically, the pancreas produces insulin, the heart pumps blood, the stomach digests food. It made sense to think that my brain generated thoughts without any intervention on my part. I surmised that good or bad, thoughts were simply something you lived with everyday. No one had ever told me there was a sorting process to go through with these incoming messages. The notion was totally alien to me.

Unfortunately, questioning the validity of our thoughts usually happens because of misery, heartache or pain. When I first realized my thinking was skewed, I was confused.

Even after I learned the distinction between negative and positive thinking, I did not have a clue about the impact of thoughts. The majority of us dismiss the concept that thoughts are important and we need to pay attention to them.

I have witnessed and participated in the following demonstration on several occasions. It is a powerful, dramatic illustration of the effects of thoughts.

The exercise takes two persons. I urge you to try it.

1. Extend your dominant arm out, shoulder high, away from the side of your body.
2. Have the other person try to push your arm straight back down towards the side of your body, while you resist. You both should be able to feel the resistance between the downward and upward forces. It only takes a few seconds. The point here is not a test of brute strength, merely a point of reference.
3. Extend your arm again and this time

concentrate on something negative or unpleasant. If you want to close your eyes to concentrate more deeply, go ahead. Again, while you are resisting, have the other person push down on your arm. Did your arm go down farther than before? Was there a marked decrease of resistance on your part, even though you were trying to resist the force?

4. Now try the exercise while you concentrate on something positive or pleasant. Put a big smile on your face. Did you notice? Your strength returned!

Thoughts play a major role in every act of your life. If you tried the exercise you had a chance to "see" firsthand that thoughts do have the power to influence intention and actions. It is proof of a mind/body connection.

The pain caused by thoughts can be emotional or physical. Whether minimal or chronic, it can keep us from functioning at peak performance. Emotional or physical pain can set you flat on your back, literally or figuratively.

Minimal physical pain can be a headache or a stomach tied in knots. Minimal emotional pain can be "feeling down" or depressed. Chronic physical pain can be the headache you develop every Monday morning at work, or the low back pain which seems to descend around mid-week. Chronic emotional pain can be the restlessness and sleeplessness every night when you are mentally reviewing the monstrous list of what is on tap for the entire day ahead. It can be the tenseness you always feel before exams, or the cycle of insomnia or nighttime awakenings you encounter every time there is a change in your routine.

As human beings we think: good and bad, positive and negative, secure and insecure thoughts. Thoughts make us happy or sad, pessimistic or optimistic, sympathetic or apathetic. They create our intentions, actions, moods, feelings, personalities and successes. Our thoughts govern our entire lives. All your thoughts, up until this very moment, have contributed to who you are today.

Academic life failed to teach us a correct diet of thoughts. No one taught us how to keep our minds clear and our bodies at ease. There were no classroom lessons on how to distinguish fear thoughts or instructions on how to change them. There were no courses on useful thinking versus negative thought patterns.

You have had mood swings and weathered them. You feel good, then not so good. The shift can take a matter of seconds. If you do not know how to turn your thoughts around, or what to replace them with, you can start to feel pretty glum. The good news is that mood swings are nothing more than thought swings. When you learn to change thoughts, you become the master of your moods.

Thoughts are the basic elements which control human beings. It is not someone else's thoughts that control you. They may influence you, but they cannot control you. Your thoughts are your own, as individual and as unique as you are.

Thoughts are invisible. No one can see your thoughts unless you choose to express them. It is estimated that we have more than 200,000 thoughts each day. Imagine if only ten percent of those thoughts are negative. That equates to 20,000 daily thoughts that work against us—20,000 murky clouds that block out the sun.

Negative thoughts make us feel depressed, angry, bitter, jealous, temperamental. They make us feel hurt, abandoned, and self-conscious. Negative thoughts turn concern to worry, fear to panic, disgust to anger, anger to resentment, and resentment to hate.

Most of the time your thoughts run on automatic pilot. Thought, intention and act are carried out without conscious effort. If you want a glass of water, you move to the kitchen, open the cupboard door, take out a glass, turn on the faucet, fill the glass, drink the water and quench your thirst. It takes no effort. You have performed the same activity countless times and it has been programmed into your brain.

There are other times when automatic thoughts block intention and interfere with action. Here are two illustrations.

Thought 1: The grass needs to be mowed.
Thought 2: I really despise yard work.
Thought 3: I don't want to go out in the heat.
Thought 4: I'll switch on the TV for a minute.

*****

Thought 1: I am supposed to meet Kelly for dinner.
Thought 2: Freeway traffic is heavy on Friday evenings.
Thought 3: I am not sure where the restaurant is located.
Thought 4: I don't feel so great.
Thought 5: I'm tired.
Thought 6: I'll stay home.

Both examples are a series of simple, separate thoughts. The first thought stated an action or goal. Subsequent thoughts sabotaged the original intent. Of course, we all put things off occasionally. It becomes a problem only when the pattern isolates us and prevents healthy activity.

Thinking IS the main process of the mind and we ARE what we think. If thoughts led us to where we are, then changing negative thoughts to positive thoughts will help steer us where we want to be. In the last few years, I have attended business seminars, classes and spiritual workshops. Each touched on the theme of negative thoughts. One speaker referred to "a wall of negative self-talk," another to "mental house cleaning." The message is plain and clear: If our thoughts can work against us, they can also work for us. If our thinking contributes to a dejected feeling, it can also contribute to an uplifted feeling. Healthy thoughts curb negativity and produce inner calm for body, mind and soul.

An acquaintance once commented, "I only have bad days in my mind." How right he is! His thoughts dictate his bad days.

The belief of mind/body healing is easy for me to accept. I learned that connection during the process of overcoming the physical and mental terror associated with panic attacks and depression. The mental activity of changing thoughts is a major part of the wellness process and is one of the prime components of the Recovery, Inc. Method.

The further along I travel on my life path, the more I realize the advantage of changes in my core thinking. My reality-based thinking is well-established. This point really came home when I attended a Silva Mind Control class. The instructor explained a technique and asked everyone to think of a single problem they wanted to solve before going into an active meditative state. After giving us some time to ponder the question, he asked for our responses. I told him I couldn't think of anything that was bothering me, certainly nothing I would consider to be a "problem."

Later that evening, as I thought about the episode, I realized my success. In my former world with my former personality, the "old Rose" would have been hard pressed to find something positive in her life.

Of course, there are still challenges to deal with in daily life. Things happen, I respond. Those initial responses of negativity, though much less frequent, will never completely vanish. I have not and will not insulate myself from the world. The key is, I have trained myself to stop, not accelerate, negative thought processes. Negative thoughts no longer take on a life of their own and control me. My inner-self no longer wrestles with events that happen outside of me. I do not panic.

Author's Note:

The Recovery, Inc. internal stress-reduction techniques in the following sections are the ones I used to alleviate a severe panic and depressive condition.

Today I use the same techniques to keep mentally fit. Once I shifted out of the critical stage and joined the world again, I faced the same stressful events you encounter in everyday life.

It does not matter if your stress is:
Slight, moderate, chronic, occasional or severe.

Or what name you use for the effects of the stress on your mind and body:

Feeling uneasy, tense, edgy, stressed out, nervous, agitated, down, anxious or panicky.

Or what your resulting behavior happens to be:
Passive and isolated, or aggressive and unruly.

The goal is the same:
Inner peace.

The guidelines are all important. You can use them in every situation you encounter. They will lead you to a fuller, more satisfying life. You can improve your mental fitness without working up a sweat.

Part Three

Overcoming Panic

10. *Dark Night—A Life Of Panic*

My first panic attack occurred while I was driving on a freeway. All at once, without warning, a thousand strange sensations spread throughout my body. I felt very hot and suddenly, very cold. My head was spinning, I was sweating. I felt smothered and choked, and had difficulty breathing. My legs trembled so much, I had trouble pushing down on the accelerator pedal. My heart pounded so loud, the sound echoed in my ears. I thought I would vomit. As I glanced out the rear view mirror, it looked as though the cars behind me were floating off the pavement. At first, I thought I would collapse. As the symptoms persisted, I thought I was dying.

Ironically all this transpired when I was on my way to a doctor's office. I was scheduled for tests because of recurring bladder infections. By the time I arrived for the appointment, ten minutes after the episode, I was a nervous wreck. I tried to compose myself, but I burst out crying when I told the doctor about my frightening experience in the car. He explained that none of my symptoms or sensations had anything to do with urology. He brushed me off, perhaps as a hysterical female. On one hand, I wanted to reschedule the test because I was so upset. On the other hand, I didn't want to leave the safety of the doctor's office. If I *was* indeed dying, I wanted to be close to someone who could save me. So, I went ahead with the procedure.

After the appointment I sat behind the steering wheel, started the car, then turned off the ignition. I was forty minutes from home. The only way I knew how to return was to get on the freeway again. And I couldn't. It was impossible. If someone would have offered me a million dollars, I would not have driven that car. That attack was the most terrorizing event of my life. The most frightening aspect was that sensations descended from nowhere.

I called in sick the next few days and rested. I

thought sleep and physical rest would make everything better. I drove short distances again, but couldn't shake the fear of having another attack. I didn't know what provoked the first assault of symptoms, and I certainly didn't know how to prevent the attacks from happening again. I had no idea it was my mind, not my body that was keeping the feelings of apprehension alive.

After a series of tests, the medical profession proclaimed my body healthy. So, I made the decision to see a psychiatrist. After pouring out my story, my first mental health professional asked if I had any history of panic or anxiety. I explained that there were no prior episodes and that this strange *attack* seemed to come "out of the blue." She patted my hand and told me I would be fine, "You're a strong, independent lady and you will bounce back." I contemplated her statement for a few seconds. But, I wasn't convinced I would have a spontaneous recovery. I knew how I felt inside, and it wasn't good. Despite telling her that I was petrified about having another attack, she didn't bother to schedule a second appointment. I thought, "Great! Now what do I do about this invisible monster that is living inside me?"

I took a month off from my job, trying to rest and relax. I do recall going back to the office one time. I stayed two hours, then left. Forever.

My panic attacks were frequent, but unpredictable. They hit out of nowhere—at church, the grocery store, the mall, the library, while visiting a friend. I was sure the doctors had missed something. Maybe I had a brain tumor or a rare form of heart disease. Surely this torture had some kind of physical cause. I bounced back and forth thinking it was a physical problem, but somewhere deep inside myself I knew there was something else wrong. But, I had no idea what to do about it. No one could put a label on what was happening to me. After many months, I finally accepted there was nothing wrong with me physically. I came to the conclusion that if there was nothing wrong with my body, it had to be my mind. *I must be crazy!*

By this time free floating anxiety had turned to high level anxiety. It was an ugly, constant companion. It lived inside me every minute of every waking hour. I was afraid to be alone and, at the same time, I was afraid to be with people. I went through spells of sleeplessness. Sometimes I slept all day. No matter how much I rested, I felt fatigued. There were times when I thought my head would explode.

Occasionally I would have a day or two of relative calm. I could breathe without feeling as if there was a elephant perched on my chest. I would spend those days sifting for clues, hoping to reveal what I had done "right" to make the nightmare subside. Several times I thought I hit on a formula, only to have it fail again the next time I tried to follow it. It felt as if I was falling apart from the inside, out.

At the height of my inner chaos, the physical symptoms were so fierce I was afraid to walk out of my house to the mailbox, a distance of 35 feet. I thought, "I'll die. I'll just die."

If you are not familiar with severe anxiety, think about an incident of stark terror that scared the living daylights out of you, made your whole body shake like a leaf, or caused you to literally force yourself to breathe. That is panic.

Perhaps it's the feeling you and thousands of air passengers experience during take-off. The aircraft feels as though it is floating, not climbing. In a single instant you question whether the plane will reach its target altitude. Your stomach starts to rumble. Your heart either races or skips a beat or two. You hold your breath. Once the plane ascends and levels off, your breathing evens out. The moment passes, but the general feeling of tenseness lingers on. That is anxiety.

Moments of panic affect your body. They cause you to breathe deeply or not at all. They cause your heart rate to accelerate and your body to tremble. Your heart leaps into your throat, tears can flow spontaneously and you speak in a whisper. You feel as though you will "fall apart."

Moments of panic leave an imprint on your mind. If

you have ever been chased by a vicious dog, lost when you were a child, had your own child wander off, you have felt anxiety and panic. If you have ever been startled awake by a crisis call in the middle of the night, or had your car fishtail on a slippery road, you have felt anxiety and panic. Situations such as these cause a great deal of physical and emotional discomfort. If you remember them vividly, you may be having some physical sensations right now.

For a moment, think about having the same sensations, for no reason at all. Imagine, no outside influences to trigger the alarm, light-headedness, racing adrenaline; the feeling your whole body will burst; the sense you cannot hold up for another minute. Envision layer after layer of sensations descending from nowhere and enveloping you. Sensations over which you have no control. They greet you the minute you wake up. As the day progresses, they grow stronger and stronger. They may subside, but never really leave completely. Hour after hour, you wonder when they will return. There is no escape. People with panic disorders live this portrait of agony. How can we endure all those horrifying feelings? Perhaps we're not as weak as some people think.

During the course of my illness I developed other fears and symptoms. When a friend and I walked along a downtown street, I often felt the sensation the sidewalk was coming up, and the buildings were going to topple down on me. For more than a year, I felt dizzy and nauseated every day. I went through a phase when I cried every day. Another phase when I cleaned. Everything in sight was dusted, cleaned, scrubbed and polished. Over and over, and over again.

There were times I was afraid of myself. I worried that I might totally lose control and harm myself without even knowing it. I felt worthless because I couldn't work, scared and humiliated because I was sick. Depression set in and I lost interest in life. I was puzzled. I was angry, at myself, at God, at anyone who had touched my life and may have contributed to my suffering. Confusion, pain and terror dominated my days and nights. I wondered, "How close am I to stepping off the edge?" I wondered if and when I would lose my sanity. Or if I had already "lost it."

One holiday season I tried to do all my shopping by mail order. Everything arrived except my Dad's gift. It was too late to have anything delivered, so I had a friend drive me to Sears at 7:00 a.m. The outing was an ordeal even though I spent no more than 10 minutes selecting a shirt and paying for it. The simple act of walking into a store to make a purchase was a struggle. For me, shopping used to be automatic, performed without a second thought. But during my bout with anxiety, any outing took all the strength I could muster.

When the expected never happened—I didn't collapse or die—I accepted the narrow confines of my new world. On a "good" day I could go to the grocery store, but only through the express check-out. I could go to the library (for self-help books) and browsed for 10 minutes. I could stop for gas, but only pumped $5.00 worth. Filling the tank took too long. I remember thinking, "This is your life Rose VanSickle! This is how it is going to be—forever and ever and ever."

11. *Four Little Words Stop A Crisis*

I took home four important and powerful words from my first Recovery, Inc. meeting: ***Distressing but not dangerous***. They were mentioned repeatedly and I could not ignore the strength of their message. These four words started me back on the path to good health because they targeted the core of my problem—fear.

"*Distressing, but not dangerous*" is Recovery, Inc.'s phrase to break the spell of *any* fear thoughts. Nervous symptoms and sensations *are* distressing, but they *are not* dangerous. The statement does not deny the existence of feelings and thoughts. It does not imply that "nervous" symptoms are imaginary. Symptoms are real. Real and terrifying. "Distressing, but not dangerous," shatters the clutch of terror and fear.

If you have *any* reservations about your particular condition, see your doctor. If you have been through a series of tests and no one has been able to put a label on what you're feeling, sit down with your physician and ask whether you might have an emotional or nervous disorder. Medical doctors may be apprehensive about making a psychological diagnosis. That is perfectly understandable. They want to be absolutely sure a physical disorder is not causing the physical symptoms. If you had excruciating chest pain and chose to see a psychiatrist before you saw a medical doctor, you would be sent for an EKG and other cardiology tests. Ruling out certain conditions is how medicine is practiced.

Because I am not a health care professional, I will not comment on chemical imbalances and whether they are the cause or result of panic. I don't know whether depression always precedes anxiety, or if mental illness is really a disease of the brain. There are qualified researchers seeking those answers.

I do know that chemical imbalances are real. I have many friends in the program who have been diagnosed as bi-polar (manic-depressive). They are on daily medication and may be for their entire lives. Their professionals play a major role in the wellness process. Self-directed care is an adjunct to professional-directed care for these individuals with diagnosed chemical imbalances. Recovery, Inc. training provides the faith, hope and instruction on how to be active, not passive in meeting the challenges of everyday life.

It is common to be afraid to reveal the depth of your thoughts and feelings. By the time I went to my second mental health professional, my fears had multiplied and the physical symptoms were more intense. My first psychiatrist told me I would recover and I didn't. My condition was worse. I wasn't willing to tell my new therapist everything about my disorder. I was afraid that if I did, he would lock me up and throw away the key. So I told half-truths. Do not jeopardize your health as I did. Be open and honest.

I agree with seeing several doctors to eliminate the possibility of a physical condition. Be a wise shopper. Your body and mind belong to you. The unofficial record for the number of doctors seen by one Recovery, Inc. member is 111. This individual certainly resisted the diagnosis of "psychological" condition. She also scanned the phone book to find the closest doctor's office and hospital whenever she traveled away from home. I did something similar the first few months I was in Recovery, Inc. I planned my routes knowing where the medical facilities were located. Just in case I needed one. My "what if's" didn't keep me locked in my home, but they were still alive.

Nervous symptoms are distressing, they are not dangerous. Uncomfortable? Yes! Dangerous? No. If you have _any_ doubt about your condition, check with your professional. One doctor had told me, "You haven't collapsed before, that should be proof to you that you will not." He meant that my feelings and sensations were "_distressing but not dangerous,_" but for some reason his words did not register with me.

People with high anxiety are constantly pre-occupied with what they feel. I always anticipated my physical symptoms becoming worse. That was a major part of my problem. I monitored everything I felt very closely. The slightest twitch in my body triggered my internal "fear" alarm. Anxious thoughts activated cycle after cycle of anticipation. I watched and I worried. If I felt a slight sensation of dizziness, I was terrified that it would escalate, and that I would pass out. If I had a twinge of nausea, I was afraid I would suffer with it for the rest of the day. If I felt or heard my heart beat, I would take my pulse. I was certain that my heart was beating either too fast or too slow, either adding beats or skipping them. I was always afraid of having another panic attack. In the past my body sensations had started out mild and progressively grew more severe. Because the symptoms were stronger, I constantly thought I was in danger.

The "danger factor" is what sets the nervous patient apart from other people. Every human being experiences body sensations. A person with no nervous sensitivity experiences a sensation and does not give it another thought. A headache is recognized as simply a pain in the head. Anxious people, on the other hand, look at the worst possible scenario. A headache can trigger the fear of a brain tumor. One thought of danger (brain tumor), locks the fear in place. Fear and the belief in danger are two factors which pool nervous, mental and emotional conditions together.

Attaching fear and danger sets up a *vicious cycle* of fear. Not a vicious circle of fear, a vicious cycle. Circles never end. Cycles come and go. Cycles can be stopped. They just seem to last forever. *Fearful anticipation*, the feeling of dread and anticipating the worst, keeps symptoms alive, causing them to escalate into panics. Through Recovery, Inc., I discovered I could break the cycle of fear that kept repeating itself.

At that point in my life I did not question if four little words would make a profound difference. Some people are skeptics and think that repeating one phrase is too simple to be effective. Trust me, that short phrase works for me and thousands of others. By repeating the phrase, "distressing but not dangerous," you terminate the cycle of paralyzing fear and *take the emergency out of a situation*. "Distressing but not dangerous," stops a "fight or flight" response dead in its tracks.

Part of the Recovery, Inc. system is to handle each attack of symptoms separately and put a halt to disturbing physical sensations *before* they reach seemingly unmanageable proportions. We are taught to *handle each triviality as it comes along*. I had difficulty with the term *trivialities*. For me, it was hard to understand that my strong physical sensations could be labeled trivial. How could a panic attack be a triviality? There were many times I thought I would die before I could inhale my next breath. I lived with dizziness, nausea, heart palpitations and the fog of depression. I believed that each day would be my last. Some days I hoped it would be. Occasionally, I prayed that I would fall asleep and never wake up. If I was to live a lifetime of fear and terror, then, I did not want to live. My days seemed filled with unending symptoms. My tolerance and energy levels hit rock-bottom. I felt weak and spent a lot of time in bed, hiding from terror, hiding from the empty feelings of depression, hiding from life. It was not easy for me to identify those terror-filled situations as trivial.

The "veteran" members who had already shed their most severe symptoms, were an inspiration to me. The fears and disabilities which brought some of them to Recovery, Inc. meetings were the same that I experienced. Common threads, our lives of agony paralleled in many ways.

One experienced member told how before her Recovery, Inc., training, she spent her days sitting in her living room rocker, staring out her picture window. That's all. She sat. She rocked. She stared. Her story didn't frighten me. It made me realize my condition was not as severe as hers. I told myself if she could be restored to "normal" after being in that state, so could I.

This individual and all the others at the meetings, were proof the Method worked. These people were "well!" They were functioning: working, going to school and taking care of families. If they viewed each "attack" of symptoms as a triviality and made progress, maybe I could too.

There were times when I absorbed another individual's feelings, by simply listening to his or her example. If Michelle, who was sitting across from me, talked about a tightness in her chest, I felt my chest wall get tense. I might have trouble taking a deep breath. It is typical for nervous people to be *suggestible* to what they hear or read. Information about any type of physical or mental problem can trigger the fear of having the same illness. If we hear about someone who had a heart attack, we are sure that it is just a matter of time before we are next on the list for a bypass operation. When we read an article about any illness, we can convince ourselves that we have that same illness. For a long time I avoided any references or reports about mental disorders.

I made being suggestible work *for* me, instead of against me. I realized that if I could be stimulated by someone else's bad feelings, I could be just as easily influenced by their good feelings and to "how" they exterminated unwanted symptoms and sensations. Instead of just hearing, I listened and learned. Instead of focusing on "This might happen to me," I focused on, "This is what I can do to become strong and resistant." I focused on wellness, not illness.

All of us are suggestible to what goes on around us. We feel good when someone pays us a compliment, we feel bad when someone shouts at us. Nervous patients are more sensitive or suggestible to casual remarks. There was a time when I became overly concerned when someone mentioned that I "looked tired." I could feel good, but my little fear alarm rang. I would begin to worry. I glared at my face in a mirror and found the haggard expression I had just placed there. I reviewed how much sleep I had in the last few nights. Eventually, I talked myself into feeling tired. When you look for signs of fatigue, you *will* find them.

I have finally learned to stop searching for all kinds of imaginary signs that I am ailing. Now when I gaze in the mirror, I always make an effort to smile.

A person with mental health problems feels an abundance of insecurities and distrust, which extend to health professionals. I explored less conventional healing methods, including hypnosis. The doctor tried to concentrate all my symptoms into the tip of my little finger on my left hand. Since I am right-handed, the goal was to put the symptoms in a part of my body which wouldn't affect my functioning. The attempt failed. It was unsuccessful because I did not trust the doctor, for whatever reasons. It may have been a true intuition or simply another one of the neurotic, inappropriate thoughts I was prone to at the time.

12. *Shaking The Fear Factor*

Distressing but not dangerous. Did I believe there was no danger to my symptoms? Absolutely not! But if the phrase could free me from my prison of fear, I was willing to give it a try.

The day after my first meeting I poured over the program's main textbook, *Mental Health Through Will-Training* (MHTWT). While looking for more information about panics, I found two more interesting phrases to use: *comfort is a want and not a need* and *do the thing you fear or care not to do*. To tell you I had misgivings, would be an understatement. Although I felt scared and very uncomfortable, I could still function? It is not absolutely necessary to be comfortable? In the past when I felt horrible, I raced to one of my few "safe" places. Or, I crawled into bed (perhaps to confirm I was sick). I was now faced with new ideas. The text suggested that I had to drive. I needed to stop pampering myself, and above all, do what I thought was creating all the terror.

Armed with these new thoughts, I nudged myself into the car to see if I could drive outside my safe zone. My body was tense, my hands shook, and my breathing was irregular. All the old "what if's" were whirling through my mind. "What if I pass out? What if I arrive somewhere, have an attack, and can't drive back? What if...? What if...? What if...?"

As I sat behind the steering wheel, I told myself what I was feeling was distressing but not dangerous. Simple? Yes. Easy? No. I turned the key in the ignition and felt panic rise from deep within me. Once again I practiced my new mantra: "This is distressing but not dangerous." I must have echoed the thought one hundred times during the brief trip: each time I thought traffic was too heavy; when it seemed as though the traffic light would never turn green; when I thought the cars in the next lane were too close;

when I felt my heartbeat racing; when I remembered I was alone and travelling away from home. Every single time I felt scared I repeated the phrase. Sometimes the four words were merely a thought in my mind. Other times, to be more convincing, I spoke them aloud.

Was I comfortable during the outing? Absolutely not! The terror persisted. I was scared and thought I might collapse. But I faced my fear. In that, it was a substantial success. I acknowledged having all the internal commotion. My objective was to learn to ignore each disturbing experience that interfered with my functioning. I was facing one of the biggest challenges of my life.

For the first time in many long months, I had a small taste of "I can..." I can function, despite the sensations. This effort was the first small step in my transformation process. My goal was to stop responding to imagined threats. I was taking charge of my life and regaining my self-respect. I was not comfortable, but I COULD. I could do the things that frightened me! There is a genuine sense of inner pride in doing the things you fear to do.

If I had waited until I was completely comfortable before attempting to face my fears, I would still be home wishing I was better, and believing I was hopeless. *It is not how we feel, it is how we function*. It takes more than wishes, awareness and good intentions to build up your nerve resistance. It takes action to produce results. *Helplessness is not hopelessness*. You feel helpless in a situation, only because you lack knowledge. Once you know "what to do," the tide changes.

Was I comfortable on my next outing? No. It took several attempts before I gained any sense of comfort. I would feel some relief from the intense symptoms, but it was fleeting. The terror would be gone for a few minutes, then it returned. Even though I read that these seesaw feelings were what I could expect, I would be discouraged, then angry. I thought, "All of this used to be so simple. Why is it so agonizing now?"

The weekly Recovery, Inc. meetings were the link that gave me the hope, courage and spirit to go on. I was constantly encouraged and taught the techniques to take an active role in my treatment, my progress, my life. There was no peer pressure, rather peer support. Others saw my potential and believed in me, even when I could not. Week after week I learned by listening to how the other members of the group tamed the terror of their symptoms.

Each time I chose to set out and transcend old restrictive boundaries, I built up my nerve resistance. This is absolutely essential for anyone with anxiety problems. Recovery, Inc. calls this, the *Will to bear discomfort*. You have to reverse your reluctance into willingness. You cannot reach past your barriers by hiding behind them. It is impossible. You must reach out of your safe territory to make headway. Otherwise you will remain imprisoned.

From the beginning, I used the term *triviality* in my own practice only because it was part of the program. When I started feeling shaky, I would tell myself, "This is a triviality." The more I used the term, the more I trusted that I could do what I set out to do. Every time I used the term I cut into a vicious cycle and made *significant* progress.

It took many real-life endeavors before dread and discouragement were replaced by determination. Facing reality and setting reasonable goals, *knowing my limitations*, was part of the process. In the beginning, I knew it would be useless to attempt a 20-mile trip or to try to drive on a freeway. I would have surrendered to the fear, because I was too scared. I set my sights on small victories, stretching my boundaries one mile at a time. Even though my ambitions were high, I learned to pace myself and not let up.

I learned to be satisfied with modest gains, proofs that the system worked. Because the gains were small, did not mean they were insignificant. Quite the opposite. Small gains serve to stretch limits. They helped me to become more comfortable when I was alone and travelling farther and farther from home. Small gains that build on each other are part of the process, the process of learning to trust yourself again. At first I avoided left turns. I figured out how to reach where I was going by making a series of right turns. That may have added time to my trips, but it also added comfort. And, I still arrived at my destination. I did not race out of my comfort zone. I crawled out of it. Each day I made a point to either walk or drive, to do something that I feared to do. Each day I forced myself to go at least as far as the day before. At first, I drove one more block away from home, then watched the odometer turn. I set my goals by it, first in half-mile, then mile increments. Each day I pushed myself to go farther away from my house before turning back. Often I would return home feeling so exhausted I would take a nap. When I recognized the naps were becoming a habit, I began journaling my outings as soon as I returned home. Writing out short details of what I accomplished helped me to keep my mind alert and occupied. The entries were only a few sentences long, but they served a purpose. They became my personal progress report. When I looked back at them, I could "see" my growth.

When I described my first expedition out of my safe zone, I described how afraid and reluctant I was to venture out. You may recall the "what if" fears prior to setting out and during the trip. I changed the fear thoughts to "this is *distressing but not dangerous.*" Then, I gave orders to separate sets of muscles to sit down in the car, turn the ignition key, and back out of the driveway. Changing my thoughts and commanding my muscles halted my crippling fear and gave me the courage to act. I did not have a full blown panic attack, only panicky feelings. They were strong feelings. But I was learning how to function again.

Over the next few weeks and months I learned more step-by-step guidelines to deal with my anxiety. *Nervous fear is the fear of discomfort.* It wasn't any specific activity or particular place that caused my fear. It wasn't being behind the wheel in a moving automobile. It wasn't the checkout line at the grocery store. It was the traumatic sensations that seized my body that frightened me. You will notice all the feelings, sensations, fears and nervous symptoms I described up to this point in the book are neatly tied into one simple word—"discomfort"— the absence of comfort.

The fear of discomfort ties directly to comfort being a want, not a need. I could go places, do things, be uncomfortable and still function. I could wait in line at the post office when my stomach was churning and my heart palpitating. The "discomfort" might *feel* like torture, but I could function. Not at a high level, but I could function. It was a beginning.

I had read the maxim, **take the ceiling off the amount of discomfort you are willing to bear**. To help remember it, I made a mental picture. In my mind, I "saw" myself with my right hand, palm down, resting flat on the top of my head. Then with a sweeping motion, I lifted my arm straight up into the air. I imagined myself literally pushing away the ceiling. (I was practicing visualization and didn't know it.) When I had the thought "I can't stand this another second," I recalled into my conscious mind the picture of "lifting up the ceiling." It helped me to believe I *could* stand whatever sensations I was feeling at the moment.

The operative word in the above statement is "willing." I had to be *willing* to *face, tolerate and endure* discomfort in order to grow and stretch my boundaries. I had to be *willing* to do the things I had avoided for so long. I had to face the discomfort. What helped me *tolerate* and *endure* the dizziness, nausea, palpitations, and other sensations was the phrase, "*distressing but not dangerous.*" **Bear the discomfort and comfort will come**. There IS light at the end of the tunnel. Do something enough times and you will be comfortable. There is no quick cure. Wellness is a process, it will not happen overnight.

I also discovered that **we get well in direct proportion to the amount of discomfort we are willing to bear**. Again, the operative word is "willing." You must step out of the comfort belt. The more you step out, the more you will grow.

Because I had to re-learn so many life tasks, I had to face enormous amounts of fear. When chores and responsibilities appeared to be overwhelming, as most things did in the beginning, I broke my day into small, separate tasks to make it manageable. Breaking each task down further into *part acts*, made them even more manageable. You can make any unpleasant or anxiety-producing task manageable by taking it in part acts. Whether it is a trip to the store or a trip across the country, it is easier to handle when you look at it one step at a time.

When a trip to the post office seemed overwhelming, I broke the trip into a series of part acts. Preparing to leave the house was broken down into a series of part acts: I stumbled out of bed, took a shower, applied my makeup, dressed, and ate breakfast. The actual drive was divided into segments, each mile, sometimes each block, considered separately.

Later, when going back to school seemed overwhelming, I broke the process into part acts: I saw a student counselor, selected classes and registered. I considered each class, each assignment and each exam as a separate part act.

Even later, when my first business trip seemed overwhelming, I took it in part acts: I drove to the airport, found a parking place, checked in at the airline counter. After the flight: I rented a car, found my way to my destination, had my meeting, then checked into a hotel.

When you think you're faced with more than you think you can handle, divide it. Fear and anxiety don't have to rule your life. You can reduce your stress level by reducing the big picture into separate frames. Rather than allow yourself to become overwhelmed and discouraged, you can accomplish "one act at a time."

I have often compared the process of my rehabilitation to recuperating from a stroke. In many cases, people who suffer strokes have to re-learn the life tasks which were once automatic. Arduous physical therapy brings back the use of their arms or legs. Arduous cognitive therapy brings back the ability to count from one to one hundred. People who master severe panic feelings must go through a similar re-training regimen.

Recovery, Inc. states clearly there are three distinct, vital ingredients for self-help therapy to be successful: study, practice and regular attendance at meetings. If you attend one meeting, once a week, and ignore the rest of the formula (study and practice), it is like running on a treadmill. You will remain exactly where you are. Devote only two hours this week towards getting well, and by the same time next week you will be back to feeling as bad as you did in the first place. If your condition is severe and symptoms intense, you will not feel noticeable improvement.

I took the "study" guideline literally. The day after a meeting I would review the chapter that was read the evening before. More often than not, I had to read it more than once. My concentration level wasn't very high. I highlighted the ideas that leapt out at me to make them easier to find the next time I needed them. I took notes and jotted down page numbers in a notebook. I learned to study in school by making my own notes on a subject, so I went back to the same strategy. I believe this "study" is exactly what helped accelerate my progress.

I have witnessed too many people who did not advance until they viewed getting well as one of their top priorities, right up there with breathing, eating and sleeping. These are the same people who questioned why they were not making progress. Getting well is a *business not a game*. The goal of improving your health must remain crystal clear, especially when you are in a critical stage. It is not a time to gamble and take chances with your life.

It is common to want results without putting forth the effort to achieve them. Face it, we haven't had much life training in being strong and rugged, especially on the inside. Before my illness, I used to think I was tough enough to face anything. With Recovery, Inc. training, now I know I am.

No one dictates the number of meetings to attend. Everyone makes a personal decision. One man who worked midnights, went to a meeting in the evening before his shift and another the next morning after he left work. During his first three weeks in the program he followed this regimen so he could make it through his hours on the job. Other people drive more than an hour each way to attend a meeting. Still others attend meetings every day for an extended period of time. You can't overdose on Recovery, Inc. training.

We are not accustomed to effort, and there is effort in growing and healing. We are surrounded by conveniences. Much of daily living has been made simple. When was the last time you added a row of 25 numbers with paper and pencil? I am not saying calculators are not handy and practical. They are efficient and I use one most of the time. In this day and age we are not used to putting forth methodical-type mental energy.

Rather than viewing "effort" in the negative light, as strain, pain or struggle, look at its pure, simple, core meaning—the use of energy. The Recovery, Inc. program gave me specific tools, the how to's, and I had to provide the mental energy to use them. If the devices worked for others, they would for me. No more "getting by," I was "getting well." I was DETERMINED!

My frightening sensations and thoughts arrived without an invitation, on their own. Repeating the Recovery, Inc. phrases over and over made the scary feelings disappear. Part of me said, "This is too monotonous." Another part said, "I don't want to work this hard." But the wise part of me asked, "What is the alternative? Do you want to continue living as a caged animal?" I had two choices. I could sit in the house, feel paralyzed and blame myself for not being able to function. Or, I could go out, feel petrified and make some headway." The decision was easy when I looked at it in that light.

As I look back I see that some of my early, ruthless conviction was, in part, a still existing obsessive trait. Whatever it was, it worked. With all my conviction, I launched the effort to remove my limits. With daily practice, my symptoms became less intense and less frequent. Instead of five minutes between each sensation or scary thought, the time stretched to 15 minutes, then 30 minutes. "I can't..." changed to "I can..." Today, because I have built up my nerve resistance and I know how to recognize and change an insecure, fear thought, it is unusual for any nervous sensation to last a full five minutes.

It is amazing how the four little words, "*distressing but not dangerous*," changed my life. Try using them the next time you recognize yourself entertaining thoughts of fear. See for yourself how one short phrase will unlock your limits.

Part Four

More Fitness Tools

13. *Behind The Scenes*

Recovery, Inc. taught me that there are four separate components or factors at work when I feel anxious, tense and experience nervous symptoms. They are feelings, sensations, impulses and thoughts. And this next piece of news was a real eye-opener: only two of those factors can be controlled—impulses and thoughts.

When I learned this information I thought, "Now, why didn't someone explain this to me when I was ten years old? Here I am, thirty-something, and just learning these important facts! In health class we learned how to brush and floss, the how-to's of good dental health. Why didn't anyone teach us about the basics of good mental health?"

At first I believed something was wrong with me because I didn't know these basic truths. I thought, "This is so simple, how did I miss it?" Well, I didn't miss the message, and neither did you. It was never presented to us in the first place as part of our fundamental educational curriculum. I would say that the greatest percentage of the world population does not understand the basis of feeling and thinking.

The following scenario includes the four separate components: feelings, sensations, thoughts and impulses. Let's say I have been home from work for an hour. I could use some exercise and the dog deserves to go for a walk after being cooped up all day. But I feel down and depressed. I also have a headache and want to rest. If I have a headache, a sensation, I cannot deny that my head hurts. If I feel down and depressed, a feeling, I can't just say, "I feel happy" and magically lift my mood. But, if I am having thoughts that cause me to feel down and depressed and contribute to my tension headache, I can change those thoughts. If I don't want to take Rover out for a walk because I am down and have a headache, I can control the impulse to flop down on the sofa.

The process of changing behavior is two-fold. First, you must form new thoughts to take control of present thoughts. Second, you must command your muscles to take control of your impulses. There is more: you only have to re-direct the thoughts or the impulses. Managing either (thoughts or impulses) will refresh feelings and sensations back to a healthy, less stressful state.

I created an acronym to help retain those pieces of wisdom. I used the first letter from the word impulses, (I) and the first letter from the word thoughts, (T) to form "IT." Remember, you have power and control over "IT." You do not have to concentrate on feelings and sensations because they are not under your direct control. Feelings change, they are not permanent.

When you have a thought that begins with, "I feel," and you want to change how you are feeling, start working with "IT," impulses or thoughts. If you begin a statement with, "I can't stop thinking about," change your thoughts. Thoughts and impulses control feelings and sensations. And YOU, only you, have control and power over your thoughts and impulses.

Do you know anyone who seemingly doesn't become rattled by life's little events? Do you admire this person who remains calm and peaceful, no matter what happens? Or do you resent him because you ARE bothered by people's comments and behavior? Being hypersensitive can be a new experience or a familiar one. Many of us can trace those feelings of sting and hurt back to early childhood and adolescence.

Until you learn *what* you can control, it is common to react to someone else's actions—whether you are at work or school, at home or a party; whether a statement is made by a friend or a foe, face to face or on the phone; whether the remark is directed at you, or merely as a passing comment; whether or not the statement is a criticism. You can spend hours or days creating a three-act drama by picking apart one simple line. While you are busy, you may stop thinking about what it is you reacted to. But as soon as you are still, your mind picks up the event again. When I was overly-sensitive and temperamental, I recognized it. I wanted to change the tendency, but I didn't know how to change.

Now that I have done a lot of growing up, I realize that by the time I was 21, I qualified for a masters degree in being overly emotional. Inside, I was easily ruffled. Most of the time, I was easily hurt, and on occasion, easily angered. I was careful to hide those feelings. My negative emotions rarely showed on the outside.

About 25 years after I graduated, I talked to the nun who had been my high school home room teacher for two years. She was young, progressive, and smart and she treated everyone with consideration. She was the first adult with whom I could be totally honest. After graduation, I visited her occasionally, then lost touch.

During our phone visit we caught up on the years. I told her about my volunteer work. (I never pass up a chance to tell anyone about the benefits of Recovery, Inc.) While talking to this wonderful soul, I mentioned having occasional nervous problems during adolescence. One in particular stands out in my mind. No matter what brand anti-perspirant I used or how often I changed dress shields, there were times I would perspire so heavily that my armpits would be wet down to my waist. The only thing that camouflaged the downpour was my navy blue uniform blazer.

My former teacher surprised me by saying that she always thought I appeared so "together" and "outgoing." She had no inkling of the nervousness I suffered as a teenager.

Now that I have insight and understanding, I realize my "breakdown" did not simply happen overnight. In spite of the fact the severe symptoms seemed to "come out of the blue," I lacked healthy psychological tendencies over a period of several years. Having finally reached a high degree of peace and happiness in my life, I realize that I struggled during a good part of my life.

Most of the time things weren't chaotic, but I wasn't

calm either. It was almost as though I knew something was missing. There was a void. I looked around at other people and thought I was different, sometimes to the point of feeling like an imposter. They were happy and carefree. I wasn't. Now I know the missing "piece" was inner "peace."

Today, I view my "breakdown" as the greatest turning point in my life. Without it, I am sure I would have continued to drift in and out of my restless inner vacuum. I would still be struggling along. The severity of my condition forced me to take action. Recovery, Inc. provided the Method. I provided the effort. I have one of the most important components of living a satisfying life: my mental health.

When I was free of the most intense symptoms, I functioned outside my home again, even though my nerve resistance was low. I was by no means comfortable. The severe "panic symptoms" were gone for the most part. What remained were chronic reminders that I "had to keep swimming to keep my head above water." If I defined the brutal panic symptoms as a 10, I would say the chronic symptoms were at a level of five or six.

After the demanding phase of a physical illness, our bodies are weak and our physical resistance is down. You can feel depleted after a hardy bout with the flu—"Well," but not particularly up to par, not one-hundred percent. You resume your daily routine, but you are careful not to overtax yourself. You may go to work if you are still sniffling and congested, but you do not go out in the cold and shovel snow. You do not run a marathon. Common-sense knowledge has taught you either of those activities would only jeopardize the progress you have made in regaining a healthy body.

Sound, practical information of what we can do to regain and maintain physical health is part of our upbringing and part of on-going life. What is missing in our world is widely-known, common sense logic regarding mental health.

I have stated before that we are at different states of mental health throughout our lives. There are times when nerve resistance is high and we feel at peace. There are times when our nerve resistance is low and we feel unrest. If you want to test whether your nerve resistance is high or low, look at how you react to the stress of your everyday life. It is quite simple. If you *are* reacting, your nerve resistance is down. If your nerve resistance was high, you wouldn't have all those spontaneous reactions to the events outside of you. If your nerve resistance is very low, you may feel as if you are about to explode, "blow a gasket" or "come apart at the seams."

Because of my mental state, my tension was still somewhat high and my tolerance level for stress was low. At times it felt as though my nerve endings were raw and exposed. I was extremely sensitive to what was going on around me. I reacted to things many other people would not have given a second thought. And frankly, I did not like the way I reacted. My nerve resistance was down and I had to work hard to build it up.

I have already described the tools I used in phase one for severe panics. As much as I believe I would not have made it out of the acute phase without my Recovery, Inc. training, I see now, this next segment of learning and practice was absolutely critical. If I had not continued to attend weekly meetings, my personal growth seminars, I would have remained entrenched in a faulty pattern of neurotic thinking. I may have accumulated knowledge, but I would have missed out on how to put it to use in my daily life. I may not have relapsed, but I know that I would never have progressed to my present state of mental health. I would not have the deep understanding of what contributes to my peace and what robs me of it.

I believe you will only find true peace when you set your values in life to include your mental health. My definition of "peace of body and peace of mind" is *mental health*. In my dictionary the words "peace" and "mental health" are interchangeable. When you are mentally fit, you feel calm, peaceful and self-assured.

The two basic retraining tools in the Recovery, Inc.

Method are to *change thoughts* and *command muscles*. All the other techniques build on these two actions. They are the roots of "what to do" in *any* situation that causes distress. As humans, we have control over our thoughts and muscles —the basic mechanisms that rule how we act and, subsequently, how we feel.

At the highest level, "what to do" is supervised by your Will. Your *Will accepts or rejects your thoughts and ideas, and stops or releases impulses*. Two simple functions, your *Will says "yes" or "no."* It makes decisions.

My Will accepted thoughts of fear and danger. As a result, my body and mind remained in a high state of anxiety, and produced an endless supply of anger, fear, and tension. I had trained my Will with illusion, not reality. I trained my brain with what I *assumed* to be real danger. With new knowledge and facts, I had to re-train my Will.

"Will-training" is the process of teaching your Will to say "yes" to healthy thoughts and impulses and "no" to those that are not. Will-training is the power of choice and healing. You increase your level of mental fitness only when you *consciously* choose to embrace what is good for your mind and body, and reject that which is not. The entire Recovery, Inc. Method is designed to help you make the differentiation.

One of our basic human needs is to feel safe. It is virtually impossible to feel "out of control" and "safe" at the same time. The mechanics of our minds allow <u>a single thought in a single instant</u>.

When your body or mind feels out of control for an extended period of time, you wonder what happened to the "old" you. If it has been several months or years, you wonder if something has taken over your life. You think it is impossible to feel "normal" again.

Fortunately, you <u>are</u> in charge of how comfortable you feel. Comfort starts on the inside—with thoughts. It is impossible to have fear thoughts at the same time that you feel safe and comfortable. By the same token, it is impossible to think safe thoughts and feel fearful.

We are programmed for survival, and your body and mind react to threats. You experience calm and inner peace only when your body and your mind receive a signal that says, "You are safe." Fear or feeling unsafe, is not merely a negative thought, it is an *insecure thought*—a threat to your basic need for safety. When you are panicky and you focus on inhaling and exhaling, you spawn a temporary feeling of relief. You cannot truly dispel fear with breathing exercises. Fear must be attacked at a deeper core level. The only way to feel secure is *replace the insecure thoughts with secure thoughts*. Fear is a feeling, and remember, you can control "IT," impulses and thoughts.

"Distressing but not dangerous," is a secure thought. When you use that short phrase, you replace your insecure thoughts, (fear) with a secure thought. Secure thinking does not simply push insecure thoughts into a little corner of your brain. Secure thoughts vaporize fear and danger. When you take away fear and danger, you allow your *feelings to fall and run their course*. If a single thought is all you are allowed in a single instant, it makes sense to work at making the majority of your thoughts secure.

Tension and relaxation are total body responses. Both affect organs, glands and tissues. Insecure thoughts bring on tension and disrupt healthy, normal body functions. Secure thoughts relax and restore them to a calm, healthy, natural state.

When your body becomes tense, your brain sends a message to your muscles that something unsafe is going on. Your muscles will hesitate to carry out your commands. *Don't strike your muscles with fear and expect them to act with precision*. This is true of any muscular action, from walking to talking. When you allow fear thoughts to control your mind, your muscles will be tense and they will hesitate to move. When you take away the fear with a secure thought, your muscles detect the green light. The "no danger" message appears, and your muscles will move. If you feel self-conscious and worry what people will think when you are called on to speak (fear), your muscles become tense and your voice will sound nervous. Use Recovery Inc.'s simple system of changing your thoughts and commanding your muscles, and your voice will sound calm.

If you have tried deep relaxation techniques, you are already familiar with muscle control. Most methods have you concentrate on a specific body part and consciously relax it. Starting at the top of your body, you rivet your attention on your forehead, eyelids, cheeks, down to your heels. What you are really doing is commanding the muscles in those body parts to relax. It is the same principle as Recovery, Inc.'s Method of sending conscious commands to the muscles to either stop or move.

Muscle control plays a big role in overcoming panicky feelings. When I felt overly anxious and wanted to bolt from where I was, I commanded the muscles in my feet and legs to remain still. If I was sitting, I commanded my foot and leg muscles to remain motionless and not push me upward to a standing position. Supervising muscles is far more effective than using vague thoughts such as "I have to do this" or "Get a grip," (especially when you have no idea how or where to get that grip). You don't need a course in human anatomy to be successful. Target a specific muscle group and tell it what you want it to do. Use general terms, "Legs, don't move," or, "Arms, relax." Your muscles take over when your brain is sending out false fear messages. *Muscles re-educate the brain that there is no danger*.

If you stop and think about it, we have all learned lessons with the help of our muscles. In some cases our muscles teach us to be cautious. When you hit your finger with a hammer it registers in your brain that you need to move your muscles and shift your finger out of the way before you swing that hammer again. The muscular act of touching a flame teaches the brain that you must stay away from the fire or else you will be burned. When you command your muscles to move, despite the fact that you are scared, your muscles send a message to your brain that the action you just performed is safe.

When you want to push yourself to do something and

find yourself cringing, *command* your muscles to move. If you develop a lump in your throat when you want to speak, tell your face muscles to relax, then your speech muscles to speak. You will prove to yourself that the act of speaking is merely uncomfortable: distressing, not dangerous.

If you long to hug your child, your Mom or Dad, but you have never been able to, command your arm muscles to carry out your intention. Replace the "I can't hug" thought with, "Okay, arm muscles, HUG!" The command to your muscles replaces the "I can't" thought in your brain. The first few hugs may feel awkward, but keep at it.

To control any impulse, command whatever muscles it takes to prevent the action. If you do not want to eat a calorie-laden candy bar, control your hand muscles from unwrapping it. Or, command your arm and hand muscles not to put money into the vending machine and press the button for a luscious peanut butter cup.

You can put a halt to any behavior you detest. If you hate the fact that you yell at the kids when you're stressed, control the impulse to shriek at them. Control your speech muscles. At first you may find yourself clenching your back teeth to keep from speaking, but in time you will become more comfortable with checking your impulses.

To stop an activity or action which is already in progress, command the muscles involved in the activity to stop. If you find yourself tailgating the car in front of you and becoming more tense because traffic is snarled, command the muscles of your right foot to let up on the pressure you're putting on the accelerator pedal. You can't make rush hour traffic move faster by upsetting yourself. Would you rather be calm? Of course you would! So work at being calm. When you're weaving in and out of traffic with a scowl on your face, the only thing you are accelerating is your tension.

Do you want to stop worrying about how many hours you sleep each night? Control your eye muscles from looking at the clock. If you don't see the numbers creep from 1:00 to 2:00 to 3:00 a.m., you won't be able to calculate how little sleep you are going to get. If you find yourself glancing at the clock, command your arm muscles to reach out and turn the clock around to face the wall. Then, if you happen to look towards it, you will not see the time. My alarm clock has faced the wall for years, and I am never concerned about how late it is, or if my body will have enough rest. I never tell myself, "I'm going to feel tired tomorrow." Try the technique and prove it to yourself.

Most of us don't realize that we become more nervous when we try to restrain an action. Your body experiences a brief stage of tension when you command your muscles to go against an impulse. The muscles are ready to move in one direction, and you tell them to move in an opposite direction. They respond as if they are saying, "Hold on, I'm confused. I was headed south. Now you tell me to head north." The tension passes quickly. It is only discomfort, and remember, discomfort is *distressing, not dangerous*.

When you are upset, confused or frantic, you may think any act is impossible, but you <u>can</u> control and command your muscles. Send those muscles an order, not a wish. The terminology is important. It means you have to send the message in an "I mean business" tone. You know, the tone of voice your mother used when she wanted you to pay attention; when she shouted your first, middle and last names before telling you what to do.

You can state muscle commands for many situations. I had panicky feelings every time I walked farther away from my house. As part of my rehab process, I chose to manage the feelings rather than let them control me. Each time I had the impulse to return home, I ordered my leg muscles to keep walking. "Legs, keep moving," I said. "Feet, don't turn around."

An important benefit comes with impulse/muscle control—*every act of self-control produces a sense of self-respect. Each* time you command your muscles *not* to act and you <u>do</u> control an impulse, you *prove* you are in control.

Each case of impulse control is a small step towards building the *belief* "you are the master," in control of your body and your mind. When you believe you are in control, you have more self-esteem.

Most of my self-respect was swept away because of my illness. That was another part of me that needed to be rebuilt. I found that when you practice the Recovery, Inc. system, you experience some fantastic side effects. I attended meetings solely to overcome the symptoms that were keeping me trapped. In addition to overthrowing them, I gained a level of self-respect I had *never* experienced before.

While writing this book, I have had to re-introduce myself to the person I was. I hardly recognize her, because I really am a new and healthier person today. That's the beauty of the Method: concentrate on fixing one area of your life and cause positive benefits in another!

14. *Watch Your Words*

The Recovery, Inc. Method teaches specific
expressions to use and what language to avoid. One crucial
ingredient of mental fitness is to stop thinking and speaking
in extremes. Adjectives only add to agony. Change the
expression "horrible headache" to simply a "headache."
Adverbs also overstate and maximize. You can say you cry
"all" the time or replace the word "all" and say, you cry
"some" or "most" of the time.

Why is it so important to drop the extremes?
Because they make you believe it is impossible to get well.
As labels do. "Depression"' sounds incurable because it
makes you think you are doomed to stay in your negative
state of mind. Recovery, Inc.'s expression of choice for
depression, **lowered feelings**, reminds you what you are
feeling is reversible. You CAN "elevate" your feelings by
changing your thoughts. Using the word "discomfort," for
whatever symptoms you are experiencing makes them more
manageable and tolerable. Discarding exaggerated language
is a critical element in changing old mind programs.

I can't emphasize enough that before healing can
take place, you must learn to drop extreme thoughts. It was
a caring soul at a meeting who helped me realize there were
certain minute portions of the day when I did not feel
completely dreadful. Once I started to really search for those
less intense moments, I recognized them. There were brief
snatches of time: 15 minutes when I spoke to my sister on
the telephone or 20 minutes when I washed the car in the
driveway. The severe discomfort wasn't constant. It wasn't
"always" hanging like a weight around my neck.

As everyone else who is preoccupied by nervous
symptoms, and consumed by negative thoughts, I lost sight
of my not so bad moments. I felt miserable so much of the
time, it seemed like always. Because I lived in depression,
nothing else in life mattered. There was rarely anything to

discuss. I either complained about how rotten I felt or I turned inward and became silent. Very silent.

In Recovery, Inc. I learned my habit of complaining was an attempt to *convince* myself and others how sick I really was. Nervous patients have invisible disabilities. I did not walk around with my head encased in a cast. I appeared pretty healthy to the average observer—but not to myself. When you live with nervous symptoms, no one can see what you are feeling inside, in your *inner environment*. It is not a visible handicap, as apparent as a broken leg. When you know there is something wrong and your professionals have not been able to spell out the answers, it is easy to doubt them and yourself. When there is doubt, you try to convince. Through Recovery, Inc., I learned to be aware of my complaining habit. And more important, how to stop it, by controlling my speech muscles.

I shut down my complaint department when I commanded my muscles to stop, to restrict movement. Impulses are carried out by muscles. My complaints were performed by all the muscles involved in causing my voice to speak the thoughts in my mind. I learned to control my speech muscles when I wanted to express how sick and miserable I felt.

Awareness came first. If someone asked, "How is everything?" I thought, "I feel sick to my stomach, my head is pounding and I want to go home, but I don't know if I can make it." Next, I controlled the impulse to speak the "poor me" thoughts. Rather than complain, I replied in a polite tone, never uttering a single word about feeling uncomfortable.

In the process of learning how to stop overstating how I felt, I became aware of what a negative slant I had on life in general. I was shocked at the pattern of negative thinking I had developed. In my mind, a half-full glass was half-empty, a partly sunny day was partly cloudy. My thoughts focused on what was missing or negative. Today when I have a 4:00 p.m. deadline and it is 2:00 p.m., I *still* have two hours left instead of *only* two hours left. I have found that you can't have peace and comfort if you rarely see the positive.

Learning to drop extremes is the first step in realistic thinking. When you omit exaggerating words, you think in a rational manner rather than an emotional one. And, when you are less emotional, you are more calm and in control. So watch your words!

15. *Stretch And Grow*

There are a whole different set of circumstances to face when you do make the decision to move forward, change and grow. My first efforts in becoming more comfortable in real life social situations came through Recovery, Inc. Some of the group met for coffee after the meeting. I declined the first few times I was asked. I was doing well to be able to sit in a meeting for two hours! Of course I did not admit that to anyone.

When I finally did decide to join the others at the restaurant for the first time, I felt self-conscious and uncomfortable. And I was still in the parking lot! My heart was beating fast, my knees were shaking, my palms were sweaty. My stomach felt as if it was doing cartwheels. My thoughts were racing a mile a minute. "What if they could *tell* I felt shaky? If they did, what would they think of me? I should have asked someone how late they stay. What if I begin to feel worse? What should I order? What if I can't swallow? What if I have to go to the ladies room? Will I be able to find it? What if my body starts trembling when I stand up to leave the table? Oh, Rose, why did you agree to do this? What made you think you could? Look what your body is doing, it is just about out of control again. I'll never be well again. I should go straight home. "

It does not take long for all these thoughts to occupy your mind. Recovery, Inc. refers to it as the *working-up process*. In fact, unless you are a speed reader, it probably took you longer to read those sentences than it did for me to originally have the stream of thoughts. Thoughts of fear are lightening fast. Especially when you have the litany as down pat as I did. Think those same fear thoughts for more than a year, and of course they will be the first ones on your mental screen when you become anxious.

To counteract this working-up process, I knew I had to start using some of the new phrases I learned.

What follows this paragraph are the original sentences from the above sample in the left column, (the insecure thoughts) and the specific Recovery, Inc. phrases, (the secure thoughts) on the right. I am presenting in this manner so you can see the *specific* replacement thoughts used to redirect my attention and stop the vicious cycle.

When I finally did join the others at the restaurant for the first time, I felt self-conscious and uncomfortable.

I was having an *average original response*. It is a typical reaction for someone with a nervous problem.

My heart was beating fast, my knees were shaking, my palms sweaty, my stomach felt as if it was doing cartwheels.

These feelings and sensations are distressing, but not dangerous. I have to put an end to my self-diagnosing.

My thoughts were racing a mile a minute.

This avalanche of thoughts, the *racing thoughts*, are a symptom too. And symptoms are distressing, but not dangerous.

What if they could *tell* I felt shaky?

I am not transparent, no one can see what I am feeling inside.

If they did, what would they think of me?

Wondering what people think of you is another average fear, Rose, the *fear of social reputation*.

I should have asked someone how late they stay?

I don't have to stay as late as everyone else does.

What if I begin to feel worse?

If I keep repeating the phrase "this is distressing but not dangerous," I will *not* feel worse than I do now, I will feel *better*.

What should I order? What if I can't swallow?

I can order coffee, I will be able to swallow. I can *trust my basic functions to carry me through*. If I need to, I can command my throat muscles to swallow. Comfort is a want and not a need.

What if I have to go the ladies room? Will I be able to find it?

If I don't see a sign, I can ask someone where the ladies room is. It is an average question, women ask it all the time.

What if my body starts trembling when I stand up to leave the table?

If I do shake, it is only a nervous symptom and it is distressing, not dangerous.

Oh, Rose, why did you agree to do this?

I am *building up my nerve resistance* every time I make myself face a fear. If I bear the discomfort, comfort will come.

What made you think you could?	I have felt a little better since I started coming to meetings, and I need to do the things I fear to do. It is not how I feel, it is how I function. Even though I am uncomfortable, I can still accomplish what I want.
Look what your body is doing, it is just about out of control again.	I am thinking in extremes again. My body isn't even close to being "out of control."
I'll never be well again.	There are no hopeless cases. It is average to think this way. Nervous patients are afraid of dying, the *fear of physical collapse*; going crazy, *fear of mental collapse*; and having to live with their condition for the rest of their lives, *the fear of the permanent handicap*. It is average to have any, or all of these fears.
I should go straight home.	I can't keep playing games with my mental health. I can choose to go in, or go home. It is time for me to reverse my *old habit pattern* of retreating. The decision to enter the restaurant steadied me.

What you have finished reading is similar to an example you would hear at a Recovery, Inc. meeting. I haven't related the details about the day and time, as is prescribed. Nor have I related how I would have handled the situation "before Recovery." That's a one liner: I would never have even tried to enter a restaurant, under *any* circumstances.

Let me make it clear, I did not use all these phrases, in this methodical an order. I am certain only one or two came to mind. When you are a novice and upset, it is difficult to remember much of anything. When I shared this example at a meeting, the other members added the additional comments.

My mainstay was and still is four simple words: "distressing but not dangerous." Those words will pull you through any uncomfortable situation, even if you can't remember anything else. They work because they change your focus and clear your thinking. The point is, one simple phrase will help you "SPOT": Stop Panic, Overcome Tension.

There are other Recovery, Inc. tools I used to cope with anxious feelings. *Feelings are not facts; they lie and deceive us and tell us of truths that are not there.* Just because I felt as if I was going to pass out, did not mean I would lose consciousness. The feeling was NOT a fact. The feeling only appeared real.

Feeling exhausted is another body sensation that isn't a fact. The tired, dragged out feeling I had throughout my daytime hours was only *nervous fatigue*, not an organic, biological condition at all. It was a form of discouragement disguised in feeling tired. I did not want to face my days because they were filled with torture. No one wants to face days filled with anxious feelings and terrifying or empty thoughts.

Everyone has confronted nervous fatigue when faced with something they don't want to do. There must be a few dreaded chores in your life which you haven't yet hired out—cleaning the bathroom, ironing, washing the dog? How about "duty visits" to relatives? They have a way of draining your vitality. Facing anything you consider an ordeal can make you sluggish. And isn't it amazing how much better you feel after you have accomplished it. You feel refreshed without even taking a nap, because the unpleasant event is over.

For several months I experienced a tired, depressed feeling throughout the day. As day wore into evening, I often found myself feeling better. Evenings were okay, because my day was almost over. It was closer to nighttime, a time when I did not have to face the outside world. Of course there was a stage when I went through the opposite. I had difficulty falling asleep or would wake up after just a few hours. Nighttime changed to the part of the day I dreaded most.

There was one "getting well tool" I deliberately left off my personal list: all the feelings, thoughts and sensations I experienced were *merely a harmless outpouring of my nervous imbalance*. The discomfort was part of what anyone who is panicky and depressed is bound to feel. I would cringe inside when someone used that statement on an example I shared at a meeting. I could voice the phrase when I commented on someone else's example, but would not even think those words about myself. Other people may have a "nervous imbalance," but not me.

Hearing the maxim week after week made me realize, that yes, my mind and body were "out of balance." I remember when I finally spoke the words "nervous imbalance" aloud in reference to myself. No one else in the universe realized what a big step it was for me. I was accepting I had a psychological problem. Once I did, I saw what I had missed, the word "harmless." The feelings, thoughts and sensations were incapable of harming me.

I was afraid to accept my condition because I thought I would resign myself to it. Little did I know, I wasn't surrendering to it. I was becoming free of it. Experience taught me that once you accept the facts of your circumstances, you are no longer a hostage. You are in charge. No longer a victim, you assume the duties and responsibilities of getting well. Acceptance is always a healthy step out of boundaries.

Through Recovery, Inc. I learned how to focus my attention somewhere else when feeling anxious or panicky. Doing something *objective* cuts into runaway thoughts. The purpose: to shift from thinking subjectively about what is going on inside, (the feelings and sensations), to thinking objectively of something outside of you. I don't know how many times I stared out the kitchen window, surveying my surroundings and repeating, "The grass is green, the sky is blue, the clouds are white." Objectivity is a form of focused concentration. And, it is quite effective!

Objectivity is not just a means of distraction. The technique will not work if you merely change your thinking to something pleasant—because there is emotion involved with recalling memories. Thinking about Christmas holidays, vacation or your favorite activity may provide a diversion, but thoughts will invariably drift from pleasant occasions to not-so-pleasant ones. Because we have been trained in opposites, you are bound to think about something or someone that "spoiled" an event for you. Then, negative thoughts roll into your thinking pattern.

Using objectivity as a means of stopping panicky thoughts means thinking of a material object in terms you can verify or measure. For me, it was good to have the same object to go back to and "see" in my mind. I chose my car. It was a Ford, grey, with four doors, four black-wall tires, full hubcaps and eight windows (front, back, side and vent). I used to remember what model it was, details about the dashboard and interior, but those memories are long gone. The point is, my objective thoughts were indeed measurable and verifiable.

It is just as effective to gaze at your surroundings and start naming in your mind what you see outside yourself. I have counted the number of pieces of red glass in a stained glass window, and all the white objects I could find in a room. On a few occasions I attempted to count the number of bricks in a wall. I have used objectivity in dozens of anxious situations and as a fall-asleep-technique.

There is an interesting little piece in the Recovery, Inc. textbook about a man who tried to become the outside observer to what he was feeling inside. He looked at the second hand on his watch to measure how long his symptoms would last. They were gone before he started to count. When I heard about the technique I thought it was too good to be true. But I tried it, and it works! Two easy techniques, doing something objective coupled with the phrase, "distressing but not dangerous," have done more for me in my lifetime than an encyclopedia full of information.

After I started in Recovery, Inc., I still shopped around for advice and read other self-help books. A few had similar theories, others had radically different approaches. The more I read, the more I deviated from the Recovery, Inc. principles and my progress stalled. I embraced the entire Method when I finally realized that I was creating the "should I do this or that?" confusion.

The Recovery, Inc. program is a system, a strategy, a process. The spotting phrases are separate but interrelated. They can be used individually and they link together. These verbal tranquilizers are the foundations for realistic, rational thinking. And best of all, they move with you. The techniques transfer over as you grow into different situations. The techniques are there to guide you through whatever you may have to face. They are useful in each and every area in the entire scope of human existence.

Any Recovery, Inc. veteran can tell you how tough it is at first to actually participate in the meetings. I hesitated to give an example or comment on someone else's. As the "new kid on the block," I was uncomfortable because everyone else seemed so far ahead of me in knowing the program. I was so bewildered and overwhelmed, I thought I would never learn all the spotting phrases.

Many evenings I sat quietly because I was trying desperately to absorb *all* the material in the program. Part of my time was spent trying to relate what was being said to my own condition. Another part was spent in mental disagreement to what was presented. When I didn't pay attention to the group, I concentrated on how nervous I felt inside. Not having the courage to join in was uncomfortable, but it was infinitely more comfortable than attempting to speak.

Once I finally took some of the focus off how I felt, I noticed the spotting techniques were really only one-liners. If I commented on someone else's example, all I needed to speak aloud were a few words. I could do that! I did not have to know or understand the entire program. I finally raised my hand and took my turn. I spoke one sentence. My voice quivered, but I did it. I picked one technique and spotted it routinely. Then I memorized another one.

Yes, I took the time to memorize. I have already mentioned that I took my "study" seriously. I agree with the majority of you in thinking we had to memorize some pretty useless information during our school years. Knowing significant dates in history has not enhanced my life. But having Recovery, Inc. life tools etched on my brain cells has enriched my life.

Spotting tools or techniques are used repeatedly during each example. Repetition is a training tool to facilitate learning. In a short time I became more comfortable because I had learned five or six different slogans. It is no secret that repetition is the key to increased learning. You know the words to a favorite song because you listened to it many times, not because you read the sheet music. Because of repetition, we have been programmed to think "Kleenex" instead of facial tissue, "Scotch" tape instead of transparent tape, no matter who actually manufactures and distributes the product.

When I made the decision to give my first example, I was afraid I couldn't do it "right." The four step outline helped. After a person read a step, I related the details. It was really rather simple. Not comfortable. But a lot easier than I had imagined. I did forget some of the details that I wanted to tell. Following the steps one at a time kept me focused. That focus is necessary.

It is average to feel uncomfortable when you are in

unfamiliar territory. You are confronted with discomfort when doing virtually anything "new," in any life situation. When you accept the fact that it is okay to be uncomfortable, you are not startled and frightened by your thoughts and body sensations. Facing discomfort is a normal part of stretching out of the old and growing into the new. Once you learn to handle your discomfort, you can handle anything.

One of the main Recovery, Inc. precepts which prompted me to actively participate in the meetings and then in life in general is that there is *no right or wrong in the trivialities of everyday life*. Each time I gave an example at a meeting, it was a trivial instance which made me uncomfortable. I felt self-conscious because I didn't think I would perform perfectly. Seeing that there was no strict right or wrong way to share an example, took the pressure off me. I did not have to be perfect, even though I was still striving to be.

There are two Recovery, Inc. phrases that guide me through *any* apprehension I may have and anything I want to do in my life. The first is, "Distressing but not dangerous." The second is, "There is no right or wrong."

I did not adopt all Recovery, Inc. philosophies and spotting techniques simply because they were part of the program. There were a few ideas that I thought had no place in *my* life, despite the fact that I knew they worked for other people. My greatest resistance came to the phrase, "all I need to be is *average.*" I could accept that situations were typical and average. I could even accept symptoms were universal and average. But for *me* to be "average," no thank you. I wanted to remain special, different and better than everyone else. It took months before I understood how trying to keep up a perfect persona was actually keeping me tense.

What is wrong with trying to be perfect all the time? First, it is impossible! Second, it keeps a vicious cycle of fear alive. Setting extremely high standards keeps you tense and anxious because you are rarely pleased with the results.

Other people have told me that they were relieved once they learned all they had to do was an "average" job in daily life. Knowing that they did not have to be extraordinary released them from trying to be someone they were not. Embracing the concept of averageness immediately launched them on the path of self-acceptance.

That is the beauty of the program. You set your own agenda. You use whatever tools work for you, and pick up the rest of the tools as you continue to move forward.

Participation in meetings has many benefits. The actual demonstration of someone else's, "How I used this" paints a lasting impression that Recovery, Inc. tools really work. In order to be prepared to give examples, I made it a point to use what I was learning between the meetings. No one ever told me, but I stumbled on the idea of using the four-step example outline as an additional learning aid. When I found myself upset and in symptoms, I used the outline to follow the steps: (1) This is what is happening. (2) This is what I am feeling and thinking. (3) This is what I can spot to make myself more comfortable. (4) This is how I would have reacted in the past. Between meetings this format provided me with a simple way to focus on what *I* could do to improve my thinking patterns.

At times, to make it an orderly process, I wrote out all the details. Putting things in black and white has always helped me retain information. Writing out examples is not necessary, or even recommended by the program. It is one of the ways I found to practice and reinforce the progress in my own life. Writing makes it register.

16. *Knowledge Versus Skill*

The Recovery, Inc. program is based on realistic information. Dr. Low was a man of science. His wisdom consists of solid truths, not claims for quick cures and overnight successes. Those of us who "live" and love the program smile when we read the glossy brochures for one-day seminars. The marketing pitches that announce that you can learn the skills to be "more assertive, handle any difficult situation, or abolish your fear forever," in one, short eight-hour class.

It is impossible, even if you do possess an extraordinary mind power! In a single class you may acquire knowledge, but skill and knowledge are not synonymous. Skill comes from taking knowledge and putting it to use. Having a skill means being proficient.

You can play handyman and switch out the drain in your sink or fix a leaky faucet, but that does not make you a plumber. You can learn a computer word-processing application, but you will not remember how to access all the features unless you use the program on a regular basis.

Knowledge teaches you what to do, but practice shows you how to do it. There is On-The-Job (OTJ) practice required to turn knowledge into skill. Practice takes discipline and oh, how we fight disciplining ourselves. Discipline used to have a very negative meaning for me. From childhood, it meant correction and punishment, for conduct or habits. Correction could only imply one thing: there is something wrong with me, which has to be fixed or improved. Today I view my personal discipline in a more positive light. I see discipline as development and growth, power and inner strength. The word discipline puts a smile on my face instead of a frown.

We don't like to confess that we lack certain skills. Many people wish they could learn to relax, others refuse to admit they can't unwind. During my life, I have fit both images. I had an internal engine that ran in high gear. If you fit the picture, you are not alone. Relaxation is an art, not a gene. Granted, some individuals learned the skill at an earlier age, so early, they can't even remember when. For certain people, being able to relax is a given. They have no idea how the rest of us missed the "lesson."

If you were raised with the idea "You can't go out and play until all your work is finished," you may be stalled in the same mode as an adult. As I did, you somehow received the message, you were not allowed time for yourself. Everything and everyone is more important. As a child, no one ever told you to take an hour and do nothing, that play time is important. Somewhere we learned, that in order to become responsible adults, we must work. And we keep trying to prove we are responsible.

Part of the process of learning to relax will involve some uncomfortable feelings and sensations. Unfortunately, the calm feeling is not going to come immediately. You have to leap past those insecure thoughts that say, "I can't," or "I'm too old." If you take a class or workshop, you might think, "Everyone else is doing better than I am."

Remember, you can read about the benefits of relaxation till there are no more books to read. But, if you don't use the tools on a regular basis, relaxation will never become a part of your life. You will never possess the skill.

Dr. Low knew that newcomers to the program would not fully understand the concepts and would resist practicing them. It is common to want to know "how" something is going to help before it does. Recovery, Inc. teaches that *belief is the last to come.* That was a secure thought for me. I didn't have to completely understand "how" the principles worked to obtain results. I didn't have to believe, I had to "use" what I was learning. There were times when I felt silly repeating, "distressing but not dangerous" to myself dozens of times per day. Nevertheless, it worked. It made me feel comfortable, secure and at peace. Full understanding and belief came only after many months of miniature successes. When you consciously work at thinking secure/safe thoughts, there is no room for the insecure/negative ones.

As children, we didn't have to *believe* we could ride a bicycle, ice skate or shoot baskets. We tried, practiced, and became proficient. As adults, our intellect stands in the way of learning the simple way. We think because we have reached a certain age or level of academic achievement, we know all there is to know. Or we think that we can figure out what it is that we don't know through some complicated process. We are not willing to accept "simple" advice, simple advice such as, "Use these four words, *distressing but not dangerous*, when you are afraid." The suggestion sounds too elementary.

The Recovery, Inc. Method is a system of practicing some common sense, simple guidelines. I made some good strides in a relatively short amount of time because I used what I learned, *every day*. I don't believe the Method will work as quickly for a person who has to completely digest knowledge before getting in motion.

I did not run on blind faith. I ran on acceptance. There were people all around me who were getting well and some who had already achieved an extremely healthy lifestyle. They shared their belief until I acquired my own.

If you think you can't be bothered with all the exercises in changing thoughts, which are a major part of this Method, remember—your thoughts are taking up space in your mind at every moment. You might as well make them more positive and healthy. It is not going to take up any more time, but it will take a little more effort on your part.

Do you think it is monotonous repeating these little "spotting" phrases to yourself? To be truthful, sometimes it is. At times I have felt like an automated machine spewing out Recovery, Inc. words in the form of thoughts. I realized, however, that I had many years of mind programming to reverse. If I was going to survive I needed to resolve conflict. The repetition was part of my comprehensive wellness program. I had a lot of core thinking to cancel out, and wasn't going to accomplish creating a new me overnight. I have yet to see a catalogue advertising replacement brain cells. We have to re-imprint our own and it takes time.

You know the printout from a computer program will not change unless you replace the data in the file. It is the same with life. Your personal life will not change unless your thoughts change. You can't just wish things to change.

Goals are good, I whole-heartedly believe in them. Do what you can to reach your long-term ones, day by day, with plenty of short range goals. Do be a realist in "when" a goal can be achieved. Practice going across the bridge at a lake before you tackle driving over the Golden Gate Bridge in San Francisco or the Mackinac Bridge in Michigan. If it is anger control you are working on, first practice on someone who is a light-weight challenge to you. Stock-pile some "past practice" working on your responses to a person with whom you are more tolerant. Then, tackle practicing on an event that happens with someone with whom you have major blow-outs.

Recovery, Inc. helps you set new guidelines and adhere to them. It can be your "user guide" to learning reality and peace. The beauty of the Method is that you can choose what area of your life to make more productive and healthy. That area may be anger control, it may be depression. You select the curriculum for your will-training.

17. *A Pause In Progress*

There is another realistic issue Recovery, Inc. addresses that is not found in most other self-help programs. After you have made some headway, there are going to be times when you step sideways. There will be times when your symptoms are stronger than they have been in a while, times when you think you are going to lose all the ground you have gained. Even though *setbacks are average*, they are frightening because they produce fear and doubt.

During a setback, you may think that you are back to "square one." But, *we never go back as far as we were*. The very fact you have new knowledge, insight, and practice in dealing with a disorder, does not allow you to go back to the beginning in managing that disorder. Also, the *return of the symptoms does not mean return of the illness*.

My setbacks always included obsessive thinking, spells when my *imagination was on fire*, with one intense thought leaping along to another. I ignored *all* my gains and was pre-occupied with insecure thoughts, "I knew this was too good to be true. This isn't working, it's all nonsense." I blamed myself for the setback, "I'm not working hard enough. I'll never be well again." The reality is that you *will* be "normal" again, regardless of your setbacks. I am grateful I was taught that setbacks are an inevitable and standard part of the getting "well" process. For me, that fact was a secure thought. Even though I was feeling uncomfortable, it was a comfort to know the truth. I told myself, "This is normal. I don't like it at all, but it is normal. Everyone goes through times like this. Setbacks are part of the process. This is not dangerous. I will make it through. I *will* make it through." Had I not known the facts, it is likely that I would have given up on the program and myself. Being unaware of facts adds confusion and fear. A setback, or lull in progress, is the reason why so many people quit so many self-improvement projects and resume the search for the "right" path.

During a setback it is typical to fall back into comparing yourself to others and feel as though you failed. It is a time when vision is clouded and the three main fears, physical collapse, mental collapse and permanent handicap resurface. Feelings and thoughts spell "DANGER." It is common to think your symptoms are worse than they have ever been. *Any* sensation (pleasant or unpleasant) that you experience in the present, is more vivid than the memory of a sensation that you felt in the past. Memories do fade. That is exactly the reason why a sensation you "feel" in the present feels stronger. If your throat has ever felt really parched, that first gulp of water can seem "more refreshing than ever before." You may even think it is the "best" water you ever tasted. It tastes like the "best ever," because it quenches your present thirst.

During my first setback, I learned an important lesson on how simple it was to change insecure thoughts to secure thoughts. Up until then, I thought the secure thought had to be special or profound. I gave an "I need help" example about how I felt "I was losing myself again." Nothing the group said seemed to help. After the meeting I told the leader that I couldn't shake the thought that I was "going crazy." He told me that the next time I had that insecure thought, (I'm going crazy) to replace it with the secure thought, "I am NOT going crazy." One additional word, NOT. "I am NOT going crazy." I used that secure replacement thought, and in a few days I was making progress again.

It was difficult to emerge from early setbacks because I became angry at myself and questioned "what" I was doing wrong. I became even more enraged because I had struggled so hard. The Recovery Method teaches that it is typical to have an angry, "why me" attitude. It is called *temper at the illness.* It is common to think, "What did I do to deserve this," and "I'm angry because I feel this way." Everyone goes through it. It is tough not to adopt this viewpoint when you cannot function at your former levels as easily as everyone else. As much as I suffered, I did not want to accept that I had any kind of mental disability.

You can have the same kind of "why me" attitude lurking inside without a diagnosed disorder. It surfaces after you acknowledge that you have any problem which requires intervention and effort on your part. You can recognize the temper at your condition, by the mere fact that you question "why" you are more prone to anger, weight problems or any of the other outer manifestations of lowered self-esteem. The temper is evident when you ask "why" you have to work so hard to correct your personal difficulty.

Recovery, Inc. taught me I did not have to be ashamed of *any* incapacity. I was a worthwhile person despite the fact that I had a mental health challenge. Once I discontinued the "poor me" routine and stopped turning my back on reality, I accepted myself as a valuable human being. A human being with a problem. My impediment certainly could have been worse. There are people all over the world with greater difficulties. Who hasn't faced a challenge?

The program did not deceive me. It did not imply or convey the idea that I would instantly recover and never again be burdened with nervous symptoms. The program teaches truths. It teaches that wellness is a process. So many people make the mistake of staying away from group meetings when they are not "feeling as good" as they were before. Perhaps they are ashamed to face the group and admit they could use some help. When you are in a setback, it is vital to attend meetings, not avoid them.

Someone once said we should accept setbacks with "open arms" because they are the times when we learn some of our greatest life lessons. That may be true, but I wish there were a more kind and gentle way to learn those lessons. Setbacks are frightening. During a setback I learned to ask myself, "What can I learn from this?" That one simple question puts a setback into a more positive light, because it shifts your thinking from what you are "feeling," to what you could be "learning." After each setback I was on more solid ground because I focused on the gains I had made, instead of the suffering I had gone through.

What I remember most distinctly during early setbacks was trying to diagnose "what" was happening to me, and "why" it was occurring. When I realized that I was back to my old habit of diagnosing, I made the *conscious* decision to practice more deliberately. Setback time is back-to-basics time. It is the time to be on guard for *each and every fear thought*, time for a dose of "distressing but not dangerous" on a regular basis. Even though a setback is a battle, it is time to carry on and carry through. My setbacks were frequent in the beginning. After awhile I stayed well for longer periods of time. Now, there are literally years between setbacks.

It was during one of my setbacks when I found my favorite chapter in *Mental Health Through Will-Training*. I returned to it so many times I finally read it aloud into a recorder so I would have an audiotape of it to play in my car. The chapter, "Mental Health is Supreme Purpose, Not Subordinate Goal," explains there are personal long-range goals in life that include career, family, and social obligations. I learned that no matter how important those areas may seem at times, my mental health is my *supreme goal*. Without good mental health, it is impossible for me to grow in any area of life. Family, relationships and career are very important. In order to contribute in a positive way to anyone's life, first and foremost your own, you have to be healthy—healthy in mind and body.

As humans, we are faced with making decisions everyday. When you live with depression or any kind of confusion, you lose confidence and trust in your ability to decide what is best. When I was in the midst of suffering I had to put ALL my energies into getting well. Nothing was more important, *everything* else had to take second place. Nothing interfered with my Thursday evening meeting time.

When you are suffering, you must put priorities in order. Meetings are an important part of the training process. You don't change your schedule to meet someone else's needs. You may want to be a loyal spectator during your daughter's soccer season, but your obligation has to be to yourself, not the person playing the game. This is not a selfish gesture. You can't play with your mental health. Once you re-establish emotional stability, when your healthy thinking patterns become more instinctive than intentional, you can be more flexible with your schedule. Then, you will be better equipped to try new adventures. Don't ever put your mental health on hold.

My favorite chapter also contains the words *all-absorbing purpose*. I take that to mean more than desire or intent. It is a *total effort*: intent combined with action, desire coupled with determination. "All-absorbing purpose" is a passion to do everything possible to attain the goal of "peace of mind." There have been times over the years when I wrapped myself up in concerns about school, work, family illnesses or personal relationships. Not setbacks, but times when I began to feel frazzled. When this happens, it may take a few days or weeks for me to realize what is going on, but then it is time to regroup. It is time for a refresher course about what is important to me. It is a time for healthy limits and balance.

I listen to my home-made tape, or re-read the parts of the chapter I highlighted. Taking a few minutes of my time helps puts things back in the *correct* perspective. For the next few days I concentrate on my mental health. I ask myself if what I am thinking and how I am behaving is contributing to my inner peace. My practice becomes a little less intuitive and a little more conscious. It is amazing how fast I can turn things around in *all* areas of my life, by simply focusing on mental well-being. I do what I need to do to take care of myself. For me there is one top aim—keeping well.

Setting your mental health at the top of your priority list is not selfish, it is healthy. Keeping that goal in mind helps you take responsibility for yourself. It makes you caring, compassionate, loving and understanding towards yourself and towards others.

18. *Create A New Self-Image*

Part of the human thinking pattern is to compare ourselves to others. When you are in a less than healthy mental state, you don't believe you measure up to anyone's standards. You need a specific tactic to make you start believing in yourself when your self-confidence and esteem are ground to dust. Affirmations such as, "I'm doing great!," are not going to work, because you are not doing great and you know it. Just because you feel down and distraught, doesn't mean you can lie to yourself and believe it.

Recovery, Inc. teaches you to give yourself credit for the energy you put forth, not any outside results. *Endorse for effort, not the outcome. Self-endorsement* is a mental "pat on the back" from you, to you. As much as we think we need appreciation and approval from those around us, it is absolutely necessary to fill most of the void ourselves.

My first thoughts on self-endorsement were, "That is the most egotistical thing I ever heard. How vain!" The last thing I wanted was to turn into one of those self-centered individuals who go around telling the world how wonderful they are. I was functioning at what I considered an adequate level, so I pretty much rejected the whole notion of self-endorsement. I told myself, "It's nice, but I don't particularly need it."

The veterans in the group were always repeating, "There is effort in *everything* we do, and we should be endorsing for it." I could not understand the effort in *everything*. Where is the effort in the little everyday tasks: brushing your teeth, dressing and doing chores around the house? These things are automatic, or should be. My definition of effort was something monumental, strenuous and tiring. I wasn't climbing any mountains, so I didn't have any reason to pat myself on the back.

Personal experience brought out the true meaning of

self-endorsement. I was in a setback, making less than perfect progress and felt as if my mind and my body were shutting down. I felt very panicky and out of control again, as though I was trapped behind an invisible wall. I needed help and I could not wait for the next meeting to obtain that help. By the time I reached out for help from a Recovery, Inc. friend, I was crying and could hardly speak.

Recovery, Inc. calls this support mechanism between meetings, a **five-minute phone call**. The caller uses the same simple example outline used at the meetings: this is what happened, this is what I am thinking and feeling, this is what I have spotted, (but it doesn't seem to be working). The person taking the call helps by spotting the fear or anger that they observe in the situation. The five-minute call is similar to an example given at meetings, but shorter. One person does the "spotting," the detecting and commenting, instead of an entire group.

Sometimes when I initiated a five-minute phone call I simply listened, other times I listened and took notes. I recall being put off and hurt when someone told me my five minutes were up, especially when I wasn't feeling any better than when I initiated the call. I was gently reminded this was a self-help program. Someone could help, but I had to spot and stop my insecure thoughts. I had to stop and think about what I was thinking. I had to spot—identify, recognize, acknowledge, and admit, without self-blame, what was going on inside of me. Someone else's spotting could add some clarity to my thoughts and behavior, but only I could work at changing them around. I had to work on my "IT," my impulses and my thoughts. I had to practice.

During this particular phone call, among other things, I was reminded to endorse for all my efforts, give myself a pat on the back for everything I did that day. After I hung up the phone, I decided rather than wallow in self-pity, I would attempt to straighten up the kitchen. Since nothing else seemed to help my mental state, I thought I would try endorsing. I opened the dishwasher door and said to myself, "You are doing good, Rose." I pulled out the top rack loaded the glasses and cups, and repeated, "You are doing good, Rose," I pushed that rack back in and endorsed, pulled out the bottom rack to drop in the flatware and endorsed. On and on.

After a few minutes of this mechanical, routine repetition, the "light went on." There IS indeed effort, energy expended, in everything I do. And when I applaud myself for it, I DO feel better. No one else has to know what I am thinking, I can keep my thoughts very private. I don't have to be doing GRAND things, I can be doing everyday activities. I can endorse for the physical as well as mental energy and effort. I can endorse for using the Recovery, Inc. slogans, for picking up the receiver and making the phone call. And I could endorse for reaching out to a person who would help, rather than impede my progress by feeding the poor me attitude.

Self-endorsement taught me to step back and be an observer, to redirect my thoughts from what I was unable to achieve, to what I was accomplishing. Even if I felt too sick and confused to participate during a Recovery, Inc. meeting, I endorsed for the fact I made the effort to attend. When you don't feel like hopping out of bed in the morning, but resist the impulse to stay under the covers, you can endorse for the effort of moving your muscles and proceeding with your day. When you go to a birthday celebration and don't enjoy any aspect of it, endorse for the effort of going to the event. When you drag yourself though a workday and you would rather be home, you can endorse for the effort. You can even endorse for effort when you are writing and your thoughts don't read clearly when you see them on paper. Self-endorsement provides encouragement no matter what the task.

Endorsing for effort provides motivation when you think you are not making improvement. When I learned to endorse for effort, there were tremendous benefits. Self-endorsement changed the tide from helplessness, to self-respect. I no longer looked for other people to reassure me that I was a valid, worthy human being.

Because the notion of self-approval was so foreign to me, it was difficult to develop the habit. Right from the start I used the statement, "You are doing good, Rose," for my personal form of endorsement. I have no earthly idea why I chose it. Now that I look at it, using my name in the statement is as if one part of me is speaking to another part of me. Some people "picture" themselves reaching out and patting themselves on the back. As with all the other Recovery, Inc. techniques, when I suggest someone cheer his or her own efforts, it reminds me to "practice what I am preaching" and endorse myself. I still don't endorse often enough today, even though I know it is a great way to keep a positive, uplifting outlook.

When I was brave enough to tackle freeway driving again, I used green signs—mile markers, exit signs and street names on overpasses, as reminders to endorse. I have had little "Endorse" signs tacked to mirrors and the refrigerator and tucked in my pocket. I have a tiny furry lion who has moved to every car I purchased since 1983. He reminds me that I am "brave," and to pat myself on the back. If you have reminders or affirmations posted nearby, move them around weekly. If you leave them in one place they will blend into the surroundings and you will not even notice them.

Self-endorsement makes you feel good about yourself, so good, that it shows on the outside. I remember having dinner in a restaurant with a relatively new acquaintance. During the pre-dinner conversation I happened to tilt my head and rest my fingertips on my neck. By accident I felt my pulse, which I instantly judged to be faster than normal, and it frightened me. Immediately I jumped into a working-up process. I couldn't decide whether to make an excuse, stand up and leave, or take my chances of passing out right on the spot. It didn't take too long before I silently went through the old litany of "distressing but not dangerous," and moved my arm muscles so my fingers would not rest on my jugular vein. In no time I began to relax. When I mentally reached step four of the outline, I realized "before Recovery" I couldn't even go into a restaurant. At that moment I started endorsing for all the effort and practice I contributed to my wellness. As I did, I broke out into a big smile. All through this private dialogue I was having in my mind, I continued to sit facing my date. I looked as if I was politely listening to his conversation. He did not have a clue as to what was going on in my mind. He must have thought my big smile was for him, because he started smiling right back. Little did he know it was my inner smile, my inner light of self-pride, which was lighting up my face and eyes.

I have already referred to the term "inner environment." It includes all that happens inside of you, the person—inside your body and mind. The flip side of internal, or inner environment is external, or *outer environment*—absolutely everything that is not within the confines of your body and mind. When I started feeling much better and joined the "rest of the world" in its activities, I expected my friends and family (my outer environment) to notice and comment on how well I was doing. It was a big disappointment when they didn't. Looking for someone else's approval was an old habit. I soon figured out that endorsement from my outer environment was a want and not a need, certainly a "nice to have," but not an absolute necessity for me to exist. Once I understood this, I realized they couldn't possibly know how much I had improved, how much calmer I felt, because they had no real idea of how much I had suffered in the past. They couldn't see inside of me before, so how could they now? I am the only one on intimate terms with how I feel and what I think. And, I am the only true judge of my progress. The peace and joy that come from self-endorsement do not rely on people or circumstances, only your own effort.

To me the two terms, inner and outer environment, provide a simple and precise answer to the last phrase of the serenity prayer used in 12-step programs: "God, grant me the serenity to accept the things I cannot change, the courage to change the things that I can, and the wisdom to know the difference." The "wisdom" of knowing the difference, is not at all complicated when defined with the clear message of what is internal or external to you. When group members "spot" what they see in an example, they remark only on what the example giver can do for their inner environment. They do not give advice on how to handle outer environment. You will not be told what to do about your spouse, boss, doctor, teenage child, car, home, pet or the local power company, even if they may be contributing to your personal discontent. *You cannot control outer environment.* You can influence and guide others, but never totally govern what people say, do, or do not do. My advice is—stop trying. Life is so much more pleasant and peaceful when you do. And you will feel so much healthier.

Endorsement helps me accept myself for who I am, no matter what stage of life I may be in. I finally learned to like myself and appreciate my uniqueness. I call it self-bonding. Yes, I have learned to love myself. And I am not ashamed to say I was almost 40 before it happened. It is a wonderful feeling. I am acceptable just the way I am. I am special because I am me, not because I am better than anyone.

If you believe love and respect are missing from your life, start being your own support team. Start practicing the art of self-endorsement. Treat yourself to your own verbal or non-verbal expressions of kindness. Give yourself a mental pat on the back, right now!

Here is a little test of self-acceptance and self-esteem. Can you speak these words, "I like who I am," aloud and with conviction this very minute? If you can't, I suggest you take note of the energy you expend in your everyday world. Keep track of every little effort for an hour. You will be amazed. In fact I doubt it will take a full hour for you to "see" what I mean. You will be tired of tallying every movement and every change of thought—every form of energy you expend. You will realize that there is effort even in mundane actions.

Before I learned to endorse for effort, I was completely outcome oriented. Endorsing detaches me from the pressure of achieving for the sake of achievement, and allows me to enjoy more of the process of what I am doing. Even today, it helps me keep from feeling negative and punishing myself when plans do not succeed. The practice hasn't turned me into being nonchalant and flippant about work. The outcome of the projects I am involved in is important. However, if things do not work out as planned, it is not a reason to destroy my self-image. I don't immediately review all the other things in my life that haven't quite gone as planned and label myself a failure (as I once did). Self-approval creates a healthy positive mindset.

We all have tasks that move to tomorrow's list, it's part of the real world. Train yourself to endorse for the effort, not results, and it will keep you from criticizing yourself for what you don't accomplish. If you have to grade yourself, grade on your effort, not your achievements. *While you are endorsing yourself, you cannot be blaming yourself*, because you can only have a single thought at a time. It is a self-defense mechanism to keep you from being entrapped in negative thinking.

Taking a few seconds to endorse, slows me down during a frantic day. It prompts me to see that I have no problems, only some challenges. Because I endorse for the energy I put forth, the word "failure" is no longer part of my vocabulary. The outcome isn't the only thing that counts. Feeling good about yourself does not stifle your growth, it fuels the desire for improvement. A sense of self-pride provides your own validation, whenever you want it.

Supplying my own approval changed me into a more private person. I have dear friends who still tell anyone who will listen, all about their private lives, then wonder why everyone around them knows their affairs. I used to fit that mold. I used to depend on others to tell me what I was doing was right. Now I hesitate to ask for advice. Usually before I do, I have already made a list of pros and cons either on paper or in my head. I do occasionally bounce an idea off a friend, but I have learned to be selective about who those people are. Some friends, loving as they are, only contribute confusion.

When you develop self-respect and trust in yourself, other people's opinions are not required. If they are offered, the opinions can be honestly assessed, then accepted or rejected. Your impression of you matters far more than anyone else's. Self-endorsement is not a form of flattery, but gentle, loving praise and encouragement. It is a sincere compliment for you, from you, to enhance your self-respect. Try endorsing for your efforts. It will do wonders for your inner glow.

Part Five

Eliminate The Core Stressors

19. *Post-Panic*

There was more to my condition than acute anxiety. Because of the intense physical sensations it is easy to recognize panic mode. Depression, with or without high anxiety, is thought oriented. And I believe, infinitely more difficult to identify. The depression that accompanies agoraphobia is often ignored. Because the panic symptoms are so explicit and consuming, most people don't even think to look for symptoms of a secondary disorder.

Although it wasn't my primary complaint, my despondency wasn't a case of feeling sad once in a while. It had silently progressed from feeling down to not having the energy to do the things I wanted to do. As a result, I felt isolated because I didn't have the stamina to do anything but the bare minimum. I constantly put off tasks which needed to be done. Either I didn't feel like doing them or felt I couldn't handle the responsibilities. It was a time of going through the motions, feeling detached and fragmented. I wasn't a full participant in the things that were going on around me. I felt worthless to the point of asking: "Who would care if I were gone?"

Once my severe panic was under control, I began to open my eyes to my life-long, neurotic thinking patterns. I recognized how much of my life was lived in fear and drifting in and out of depression. For those of you who haven't stopped functioning because of a problem, this is where you may be—shifting up and down emotionally, having trouble securing a handle on what is wrong, and how to fix it.

During the span of my Recovery, Inc. training after the severe panics were under control, I took advantage of talking to the more experienced members. I timidly asked numerous "Did you ever..." questions. "Did you ever feel lonesome in a room full of people? Did you ever feel so pre-occupied that you couldn't understand what someone was saying to you?" Every time I voiced a concern because I thought I was unique in what I was feeling or thinking, someone reassured me that I was not alone. Mine was not the worst case ever. Neither is yours, though it is common to think so.

I had tried talking about some of my feelings and fears to family and friends outside the program. Those conversations only ended up with me being frustrated and angry. I know now that persons who haven't been through a similar life situation, simply have no idea of how it feels. They may have love and compassion. But it does not come across in comments such as: "Snap out of it," or "Just get over it" or "You'll be fine." Relatives and friends only make those statements because they don't know what to do any more than we do. I quickly learned to confine my questions to the people I considered Recovery, Inc. veterans. It didn't matter to me if they had been in six months or six years, to me they were experienced. They had first-hand knowledge of the problems and the solutions.

Because of my own insecurities, I thought I might be pestering the other members with my questions. They always assured me I wasn't. I was following the three vital guidelines for self-help therapy: I attended the meetings, I studied Dr. Low's works, and I used what I learned in my every day life. The experienced members were glad to help.

This early practice of speaking up and asking questions made me more comfortable in all other areas of my life. Today I do not hesitate to ask for an explanation of what I don't understand. Yes, I occasionally run into people who believe they are intellectually superior because they know something I don't. They are a real part of life. Now, however, I don't allow them to intimidate me.

20. *Many Faces, Many Names*

Basic emotions are not complex, but they are often disguised. During my wellness process, I worked on them separately, but simultaneously. In the process of reducing fear, I uncovered a lot of hidden anger. Once my anger was exposed, I made a conscious and concerted effort to recognize it. The body and mind reactions to anger and fear are the same. The management techniques to combat anger and fear are also the same.

Fear is a very private, internal process. We are taught at a very young age to be tough and hide our fear. When you feel fearful, you don't feel strong, you feel weak. Feeling you are weak or incompetent feeds the vicious cycle of fear. Fear isn't only horror, panic and alarm. In more subtle forms it shows its face as worry, self-blame, feeling embarrassed or ashamed, wondering what other people think of you. *Fearful temper* is how it is defined in the Recovery, Inc. program. In simple terms, it is being angry at yourself. Fearful temper is judging yourself wrong for something you said or thought, did or did not do, or thinking you are not up to par with the rest of humanity.

The opposite of judging yourself wrong is *angry temper*: placing the blame on someone else for something they said, did, or did not do. The explosive variety of anger is easy to identify. We have all seen at least one example of someone vibrating with rage and taking it out on a waitperson, ticket agent, salesclerk or bank teller. There is the person who honks the horn and screams at the driver ahead because he hasn't decided to turn right when the traffic light is red. This irritated person believes the law reads right on red is "required," when in fact, it reads that a right turn is "allowed" on red. The person first in line at the intersection makes the judgement call.

Anger too, has many faces and many names. You can feel annoyed, irritated, insulted or humiliated. A private affair with angry emotions is more difficult to distinguish. Those of us who were taught not to be angry, learned to say "our feelings were hurt."

Humans have two basic predominate dispositions they act on when they are uncomfortable—fight or flight. Some people react outwardly to fear and anger, others retreat. Both instincts are normal reactions—one is external, the other internal.

If you are a person who verbally rants and raves, is aggressive or stomps around when you feel angry, it is going to be more difficult to be aware of your fear temper. If you are a person who internalizes your feelings, is more sullen and passive, it is going to be more difficult to be conscious of the angry temper. We all display some of each behavior and most people have a dominant disposition to operate in one way or the other. There is one temper closer to the surface, another you will have to search for.

If your dominant predisposition is out of hand and is ruling you, the bad news is you will have nervous symptoms. Whether you are shouting on the outside or the inside, you will have problems. The good news is you can learn to moderate your reactions and bring calm, peace, stability and spontaneity back into your life.

Some people have a tendency to overreact, for whatever reasons. A person who is suffering from a nervous or emotional problem is sure to overreact. Or sometimes they have no reaction at all. That, too, is overreacting, the other end of the spectrum. Neither the explosive nor the non-reaction is healthy. In Recovery, Inc., we are taught to distinguish between the two, and operate within healthy guidelines.

Dr. Low found our responses to fear and anger generate the same affects on our bodies and our minds. He referred to them with one term: *temper*. Fearful temper and angry temper, standing side by side or alone, are what cause our tension and stress. The tension, in turn, generates the symptoms—the unrest in our bodies and our minds. *Temper causes tension and tension causes symptoms*. When we use the term "temper" in Recovery, Inc., we refer to both anger and fear.

The most common immediate responses to thinking you have made a mistake are blushing, a body reaction, and a feeling of embarrassment, a fearful thought response. The most common immediate responses to anger are an overall feeling of tenseness, clenched fists, or tight shoulder muscles. If you keep up the pattern of angry or fearful thoughts, more of your body becomes tense. Tension causes jittery hands and wobbly knees, upset stomachs, neck pain, optical migraines, and colitis, lack of concentration and racing thoughts—the mind chatter, the internal dialogue, the tape entitled, "What If," running wild in your mind. Yes, those racing thoughts are a symptom. They keep us re-living the past and dreading the future. Most of all, the racing thoughts keep us from living life to the fullest in the present.

In my view, the absolute worst feeling a human being can have is to "feel out of control." Body sensations or obsessive thoughts, when you feel they have taken over, you are alarmed, anxious, fearful and frightened. That is one of the reasons fear of public speaking is at the top of the social phobia list. Standing in front of a group of people is the trigger for the fear. The real fear is of not being in control of those body sensations—the trembling hands and rubbery legs, the twitch in your neck and face muscles, the inability to smile a broad relaxed smile. Uncomfortable body sensations seem to take on a life of their own.

Ask anyone what the most difficult thing they have ever had to do, and I bet they describe feeling "out of control." The most uncomfortable situation is always the most difficult situation. They probably will not use the word "fear" or admit "feeling out of control," but it will be the crux of what they were thinking. Most people I have quizzed on the subject tell about a public speaking experience.

The most universal feeling of being out of control is probably crying. Not many people can relax and let the tears run down their face. Most everyone can recall at least one incident which caused physical or emotional pain—a time of spontaneous tears and deep sobs—from a broken bone or a broken heart. The loss of a loved one generates tears and so can a broken wrist. During my depression, I had a spell when I cried several times a day, every day. Today I can't remember the triggers, only the tears. I do recall feeling "out of control" and thinking, "I'm losing it." It is common to feel scared and "out of control" when you can't subdue what is going on inside of you.

Situations that are beyond your control also make you feel "out of control." Because you can't take command, the result is fear and anger. The event can be as insignificant as a traffic tie up, or as serious as an illness that is gripping you or a loved one. In these situations we often try to change what is happening outside. What we need to do is maintain order at an inner level. And that is precisely what we have not been taught. You cannot be expected to effectively act on what can be altered, when you do not have the knowledge.

You can also feel "out of control" when thoughts become lodged in your mind. I had to fight off obsessive thoughts during my depression, but there were other times when an idea lodged in my mind and took over. For a long period of time when I was 20, I was afraid I would die before my twenty-first birthday. In my era, 21 was the magic age when you became an "adult." There was no rational reason for the thought. No looming physical illness, not really any physical sensations I can recall. Just the thought, "I'm not going to make it." Of course it unnerved me, mostly because it repeated itself so frequently and I couldn't make it go away. The thought came several times a day for many months. I wondered where it was coming from and why it chose to possess me. I never heard of anyone else preoccupied with thoughts of death, so I thought I was strange. And, of course, I told no one. After the birthday finally came and went, the obsession left me. Today, because I know how to swap out my insecure thoughts, my thinking never grows to the point of an obsession.

Recovery, Inc. principles teach you to be *self-led rather than symptom-led*. Skeptical, pessimistic fear thoughts do not have to rule your life. You regulate your thoughts.

21. *Camouflaged Temper*

Recovery, Inc. addresses two other thinking/behavior patterns I would have never considered forms of "temper" (anger or fear), in their standard definitions: comparing, and rushing.

Comparing is temper because it is a judgement of right and wrong. When people with low self-esteem compare, they usually conclude that they are "not as good as," a fear which translates to: "I am wrong because I am lacking." There is subtle anger involved because other persons are perceived to be better looking, better educated, better off financially, more socially adept. It is a game where you go from thinking you are superior to fearing you are not as good as the next person. There is no real need to dominate or be better than anyone else. If you can look at others, aspire to be like them, and work toward a goal, that is healthy. It is comparing plus reaching for an outcome. To compare for the sake of comparing, is an unhealthy habit; you are doing it to fill your time. I have reached a point where I no longer compare—which leaves me free. Free to be me. The only person I am better than is the person I used to be.

All the time management courses which have evolved are proof we all feel as if we are rushing through life without enough time. Moving and acting rapidly are caused by feeling anxious and impatient. These feelings, as any others, are provoked by thoughts. We rush because we think we don't have enough time to do all that needs to be done. But, both fear and anger are behind the rapid pace. You can blame yourself for taking on too much, a fear thought. Or you think someone else is responsible for the fact that you are facing more than you are capable of handling in a given time frame, an angry thought.

When you find yourself rushing to take the children to gymnastics class and wonder why you agreed to add this task to your already busy schedule, there is a fear thought behind your fast pace. The judgement that you are wrong for taking on the responsibility. If you are upset because your mate never has time to help taxi the youngsters around, that is an angry thought, a judgement that he is wrong for his lack of involvement. If you are rushing to meet a deadline at work, you're either angry that the manager gave you a next-to-impossible deadline (an angry thought). Or you're afraid that you won't complete the assignment within the allotted time even though you agreed to it (a fear thought).

We are impatient when we judge that someone isn't doing their job correctly. We have all stood in lines thinking the person at the front could take tickets or ring up a grocery order and count out change a little faster. Your body shows you are eager when you start to rock from foot to foot, cross and uncross your arms. Waiting in line is part of life. You cannot rush when you are forced to stand in one place. When I am delayed I try to remember it is my chance to relax, one of few in a hectic day. It is a secure thought which changes my attitude. I view the few moments as a gift, rather than an opportunity to become irritated. Inner peace—that is my goal. Change your attitude about having to wait and you will see it make a positive difference in your days.

Rushing always creates tenseness. You will not feel calm, relaxed and peaceful in your mind and in your heart if your body is in hurry mode. If you trot instead of walk, slow down those leg muscles. I guarantee you will feel more calm on the inside. I still catch myself moving at a quick pace. I must think the milliseconds I am saving will add up to quality time for myself at a future date. It is possible to walk at a brisk pace and relax at the same time. It is quite different from being motivated because you are anxious.

22. *The Cycle*

We are a species that interact as families, co-workers, friends, lovers and adversaries. I have talked about Recovery, Inc.'s philosophy of trivialities and techniques with regard to when fear comes after the symptoms. Next comes an even more important life lesson, keeping nervous symptoms away <u>while</u> interacting in the world. This is the part of the Recovery, Inc. program, that I believe can benefit every person on our planet. I call it Life Management in Life School—how to handle stress.

Everyday life is full of irritations, frustrations and disappointments. I wish you could hear the matter-of-fact tone that is used when that phrase is verbalized. There is no inflection of fear or bitterness, merely a statement of fact. Whatever upsets you and causes stress can be classified as an irritation, frustration or disappointment. As humans, we are going to have responses to real life stresses and frustrations. That is a fact. We do not live in Heaven, and we are not angels.

Since I was irritated and frustrated a good part of the time, this was not news to me. What was startling was to learn that there were separate stages that turn a response into a seemingly unending reaction. The *original response*, the first trigger, often comes from outside of us—the outer environment. First responses are perfectly normal. You cannot control their arrival because they plant themselves in a fraction of a second. What follows are more thoughts, the culprits that cause stress and tension. The first response plus the thoughts that follow make up the *immediate-effect*, a time when you are probably not thinking too clearly. Then comes stage three, a time when we can reflect on what is going on. In Recovery, Inc. it is defined as the *after-effect*. After-effect is the stage that we can control and change. Recognizing your thinking in the after-effect stage is extremely important. If there were no after-effect stage, we would have no stress-management programs, no anger workshops and there would be no reason for Recovery, Inc. meetings.

Here is a short illustration of the three stages. Imagine that you are sitting, peacefully engrossed in what you are doing, and someone taps you on the shoulder from behind. The startle causes you to immediately flinch, or turn around to see who it is. If you like who you see, you may smile. The original response to the tap on your shoulder is a startle. The immediate effect is the automatic movement of your body, the flinch. In a split-second after-effect you realize there is no threat, and you smile. End of response.

Let's change the picture a little. You are concentrating, someone taps you, you turn around and you are angry because you have been disturbed. There is fire in your eyes and a scowl on your face. The original response is the same, the startle. This time the immediate effect consists of flinching, plus the anger and the stern look. You may not vocalize how you feel, but your body language shows you are not happy. *Features and gestures speak*, and can be more menacing than words.

Next comes the after-effect, the run-on thoughts. If your thoughts are "I'll never finish this if people keep bothering me," or "I should have closed my door" or "I should have found another place to try to relax," you are following your original response with an after-effect of fear thoughts (you are wrong). If your thoughts are, "This is the fifth time someone has broken my concentration" or "I never have any time to myself," you are following your initial response with an after-effect of angry thoughts (someone else is wrong).

It is very rare that an after-effect is pure fear or pure anger. It is more apt to be a combination of the two. One may outweigh the other, but 99 times out of 100, both "tempers," fear and anger, are involved. Because I seldom exploded into a rage, I classified my thoughts as all fear and no anger. Many people think the opposite, that they have no fear, only anger.

After-effect time is when you can decide, yes decide, whether to continue to **work up** the original response, or **work it down and drop it**. The working-up process is similar to the old cliché of making a mountain out of a molehill. From personal experience, I know if you keep "processing" an incident, you can create an entire mountain range.

The initial response is a simple response that causes minimal discomfort, uncomfortable feelings in the body or mind. Add the working-up process during the after-effect and you have more discomfort and tension. The more angry and fearful thoughts, and the more time you add to the after-effect, the more physical and mental unrest you will experience. The symptoms you feel will become more intense or you will be visited by others. Before I knew this uncomplicated logic, I thought that in order to gain some control in my life, I should never have first responses. I had the preconceived idea (as millions of you), that once a response surfaced, everything that followed was automatic, unconscious and spontaneous.

It is a simple equation: temper (anger and/or fear) is manifested as tension, and tension produces symptoms.

Temper(fear/anger) → Tension → Symptoms

This is another sample of fundamental reality and universal law that is not part of education. One plus one always equal two; the sun always rises in the east; anger and fear always cause discomfort. Anger and fear also undermine your self-esteem because they make you feel "out of control."

A mind is rarely without thoughts. Becoming aware of your personal after-effect process is somewhat of a challenge. More times than not, especially for rookies, we are in symptoms before we even think about examining our thoughts for fear and anger. Even after we learn the separate elements of the cycle, we do not always realize we are processing an event. After all, we're just thinking.

Recovery, Inc. spotting techniques, such as,

"distressing but not dangerous" and "comfort is a want, not a need," are the central components for relieving stress, tension and symptoms—exactly what makes them essential to everyone. Each phrase focuses attention on self-help, *what you can do for you*. And they are directed at the root of the problem. Once you know that temper causes tension and tension triggers and sustains symptoms, it is common sense and logic to work on the root—the two tempers, anger and fear.

In other words: **All stress and tension are caused by two factors and two factors only—FEAR and ANGER.**

That statement is a very important piece of information. I know the cause of *all* tension. Now you do too. It is the simple law of cause and effect. The cause is fear and anger; the effect is unrest—no matter what label you give it or how severe it is. The only way to change the effect is to eliminate the cause.

If we are going to live in a healthy society, it is essential to share this cause/effect information with everyone, especially children. We can't keep secrets. People have to know exactly what to correct before they can initiate change. With the correct information we can practice a preventive, rather than corrective approach to mental fitness.

When I quiz myself on why am I feeling edgy, out of sorts, anxious, fatigued, restless or any of the other hundreds of names we give to negative, unpleasant, unwanted emotions and feelings—I look for fear and anger thoughts. The list of what to identify is not long and complicated. You don't have to wrestle with stress management, you only have to identify fear and anger.

There are times when I don't catch the fact that I am working a situation up in my mind. Most times, however, I do. I know for a fact, that the sooner I stop and spotlight what is going on with my thoughts, the less stress and tension I will experience. Temper is toxic. Like slow-acting poison it corrodes your mind and body. If you find yourself thinking, "I feel so tense and I don't know what is causing it," take time to look for hidden fear and anger. Don't be surprised when you find an overabundance.

When you feel anxious or panicky, the first order of business is to cut into the fear and danger you are connecting to what you are feeling. When you feel scared in a situation or apprehensive about an upcoming event, you must change the insecure thoughts to secure ones. By telling yourself that the feelings are only distressing, you begin to recognize them as that. You cut into the seemingly endless cycle of thoughts that are screaming, "I'm scared! I'm scared! I'm scared!" Breaking into the danger cycle clears your mind enough to think more rationally, more realistically. Then, examine if there is anything else happening in your thoughts that has to do with being angry at something (a situation), someone or yourself. Remember playing "I spy" when you were a child? Instead of a playmate asking you to look for something red, blue, round or rectangular, this process involves searching on the inside, at your thoughts.

Fear and anger are the number-one obstacles to emotional, physical and spiritual health. Ancient and popular theories espouse the belief. Healers and religious leaders across the world have been preaching it for centuries. If you want to live a truly healthy, peaceful, and successful life, freeing yourself from fear and anger is more than a practical aspect, it is fundamental. So many people are supporting the belief, perhaps it is time for you to acknowledge the fact that fear and anger are destructive to you.

You can try all kinds of other methods to rid yourself of stress and agitation. You can watch motivational videos, take relaxation or yoga classes, run, exercise, meditate, listen to self-healing tapes, use aromatherapy, sit under colored lights. But these will have a transient effect. When you resume thinking fearful or angry thoughts, your stress will return. I guarantee it.

Dissipate your fear and anger FIRST, and the various relaxation techniques will elevate your feeling of calm. It is so much easier to slip into a quiet mind when the phony issues of right and wrong are erased at the conscious level.

If Recovery, Inc. had been billed as a course in anger-management, I would have never bought into it. As a result I would have missed out on so much knowledge. In a manner of speaking, I was forced to explore and adjust personality traits I never believed I possessed so strongly. That is another one of the advantages of the Method. I was propelled to look at the entire Rose. In the process, I found a few hidden thorns. Thank God. I would have never healed who I really was inside.

Along with being Ms. Perfect, I was Ms. Moody. My anger was a silent exchange. There are only a few people in the universe who have witnessed my fury. I was a silent reactor, an expert at carrying on any kind of dialogue in the privacy of my own mind. I was apt to answer "What's the matter?" with "Nothing." I was so talented, I needed no one with me to have a conversation, debate, quarrel, altercation or argument. I had my temper tantrums all right, but I kept them locked inside my mind. You have heard the definition, depression is anger turned inward. From first-hand experience, it is true. When I was angry I choked it back and walked around either sullen or preoccupied.

An after-effect doesn't necessarily have to follow immediately after the trigger. In many instances, I put off the working-up process until I had time for it. If you think that is ridiculous, think back to a time when you left work, a party or meeting, and started reviewing the occasion on the ride home. During that review process you began judging what went right and wrong. If you become the slightest bit agitated while you examine a past event, no matter how recent that past event is, it means you are in the working-up process.

I don't have to experience a strong first response to go into after-effect. It can be a few thoughts here and there that persist for a time, go away, then return. The thoughts are not consciously stuffed away. My mind becomes engrossed in something else. This subtle after-effect takes the most effort to recognize. The symptoms, fatigue or a dull headache, are not as glaring or alarming.

I have finally set a rule. If I estimate it is at least the third time the lingering thoughts reappear, I take the time to spot on them. If it is Thursday and my mental check tells me I have thought about something in a not so positive light on the past Tuesday and Sunday, it is time to spot. I stop and think about what I am thinking. I press the pause button on the tape player, then take a few minutes to look for the tempers that are at the base of the mild, but nagging unrest.

I am convinced you cannot improve your mental health by filling your life with so many activities you don't have time to think. Ignoring difficulties with a hectic schedule does not make them disappear. The troubles will resurface.

If you find yourself agitated and moody the minute you wake up in the morning, take the time to look for unresolved anger. Remember, it is temper that causes tension and tension that causes your symptoms. You can change your sour, cranky mood by slowing down your muscles, and taking the time to unveil your concealed temper. If it is fear you recognize, excuse yourself. If it is anger you recognize, excuse the other person(s). Resolve your unrest as soon as possible. When you choose to cultivate the feeling of calm, you will be calm.

It doesn't matter if your predominant trait is to express anger or suppress it, or if you can even identify a leading trait. It makes no difference if you identify more with fear or anger. The tools to manage and cope with them are the same. The tools can reduce the stress and tension in your world, then eventually eliminate a majority of it.

23. *Identifying The Cycle*

The Recovery, Inc. program stands for balance in what we think and how we act. If you need to curb angry outbursts or learn how to speak up when you are afraid, you need to identify the source of what upsets you. We don't delve into a subject like fear when everything in life seems to be going well. Most people do not realize that all negative thoughts are really thoughts of fear. If you think you are never afraid, read on.

If there is stress or tension in your life, you live with fear. If you are depressed or angry you live with fear. If you are anxious and have panics, no one needs to tell you about fear. You live with it every waking moment of everyday. There is a good possibility you even dream about it.

Many individuals dread a visit to the dentist, some would even rate it as terror. It's okay to dislike going to the dentist. It is pretty common. How many of you put off, or flat out refuse to make an appointment, even when you know it is in your best interest. You are scared, but you say, "I'm just uncomfortable." Anything you label as "just uncomfortable," is a subtle form of fear.

Consider a scenario when you have to tell someone something you are sure they will not be overjoyed about: you have to tell your mother you will not be coming home for the holidays. You are an adult now and you have based your decision on what you want to do. But it is the first time the entire family will not be all together. Will Mom understand? How long do you put off making that phone call? How many times do you call and make no mention of your decision? How many calls do you make and drop hints about how busy you have been at work? Do you feel a bit queasy even while rehearsing what you will finally say?

Some of us continually rearrange our personal lives, disappoint ourselves and our families by cancelling our plans to accept extra work activities. All because we fear what might happen if we tell our supervisor, "NO."

There is trepidation, a mild form of fear, in play if you are uncomfortable declining a request or invitation from someone special. As much as you enjoy someone's company, you may have no desire to shop for a baby gift, go to a pro hockey game, see a romantic movie or watch a mystery film. New relationship or old, it doesn't matter. If you ask yourself "What are they going to think of me when I say, no thank you?" that question is an expression of fear. You wouldn't be asking, if you thought the answer was: "They'll think I'm wonderful."

Being conscious of other people's feelings is normal and healthy, in any kind of human relationship. If you are the type of person who has absolutely no qualms about saying no to someone, perhaps you do not really consider that person special.

There are so many other forms of fear which are not blatant, occasions that don't flash "FEAR, FEAR, FEAR," in bright neon letters. Here are a few more samples.

Do you have your family over for dinner once a year? Only on a special occasion? Do you become a little hyper? Cranky? Perhaps you suffer a migraine, but don't know or won't admit to what is causing the pain. Or, do you simply complain about all the details that have to be taken care of? It doesn't matter if you are the parent, child, sister or brother. You want everything to be special. In your mind, everything has to be as good or better than your best memory. You say things such as this to yourself: "I should have more than two desserts. What if someone doesn't like what I prepared? What if something goes wrong? What if the roast isn't done on time? What if, what if, what if." Each "what will they think" is another instance of fear.

If you are a repair person, do you become perturbed when you expect to install a replacement part and the wrong part is delivered or find another component is defective after you have replaced the first one? It doesn't matter if it is auto or computer parts, you are afraid of what the customer is going to think if you do not meet the deadline.

Professionals list the following as the most common social phobias, high to low, fear of public speaking, eating in public, writing in public. Think about these scenarios involving subtle social fears. Do you ever have conversations with yourself prior to a social engagement, something on the order of: "I wonder if there will be a big crowd? I hope I see at least one person I know. I don't know what I'll do if this doesn't go well. Will he, she, or they like me? Will I like them? I wish I had not agreed to do this." A little apprehension? A little fear!

Have you given up trying to attend a concert, the movies or the theater alone because you feel self-conscious? When you shy away from what you believe are "couples events," it is not the fact that you will be alone that makes you uncomfortable. It is your insecure, fear thoughts that make you uncomfortable. When you wonder what everyone else thinks because you are by yourself, you are thinking fearfully. When you feel sorry for yourself because none of your friends want to join you, and you fall into the "poor me, nobody loves me" mode, you are thinking fearfully. If you feel unloved or unwanted, you feel fear. Believe me, if you do attend an event solo, and if people do notice you are partnerless, they are probably wishing they had the poise to go places alone and not care what other people think.

You can overshadow all the enjoyment of any activity with fear thoughts, whether it is a party or a church service. It is difficult to live a happy, successful life when you feel insecure and threatened.

Fears can manifest themselves in reverse of typical fears. There are people who feel out of control when they are not in the driver's seat, literally and figuratively. Some individuals can drive a car, but panic when they are a passenger. There are people who feel more comfortable in charge of a group than being one of the participants. Be it Weight Watchers, PTA or Rotary International, they would rather lead than follow. If being in the audience bothers you because you are not directing, you are uncomfortable (fearful) because someone else has the questions and you may be unsure of the answers. If you were in charge, you would have the script and there would be fewer surprises.

The reality is: *you are in control no matter what role you play*. The single factor you have complete control over is your inner environment, all that is happening inside your body and your mind. You simply haven't learned how to activate that in-power.

Speakers, from psychologists to ministers, talk about Fear of the Unknown, the fear that sets limits and stifles growth because people are unsure of what they may have to face.

You cannot conquer a fear until you know what it is. The Recovery, Inc. program provides a precise and simple definition for what the so called "unknown," actually is. The "unknown" is nervous fear. *Nervous fear is the fear of discomfort.*

We are afraid of the "discomfort" of our inner experiences. We fear what we feel inside when we are faced with a new situation and we don't know all the rules. The one and only reason we are apprehensive and afraid to do anything in life is because it might make us feel uncomfortable. It is not elaborate or complicated. We are afraid of feeling afraid.

"Unknown" means not disclosed or identified. Once something *is* identified, it is no longer an unknown; when you have the answer, there is no longer a question.

I have no limits in my life because I have the answer—I know I may have some symptoms, but I do not need to be comfortable to function. I have changed the question: "What if I am *uncomfortable?*," to the statement: "*What if* I am uncomfortable!"

The opposite of not knowing, is knowing. Whatever I choose to do, whatever paths I choose to walk, there may be challenges. The challenges may involve some discomfort, some uncomfortable feelings, but they are only feelings. I have the power to form thoughts and revise them, accept or reject them, and command my muscles. Nothing is beyond my reach. "What if's," can't scare me anymore.

If you insist you have no fear, look closely at what you speak and what you think. Every time you think or say, "I can't..., I wish I could...," or "I could never do that," in effect you are saying, "I am afraid." You are setting limits on your growth and eroding your self-image, by voicing fear.

Simply change the "I wish..." or, "I can't..." statements to "I can..." or, "Someday I will..." Drop the "never," and you immediately remove the danger, the insecurity that is holding you back. In a very small way you will begin to believe that what was once unattainable, is at least possible. It is a process of tossing out one thought for another—changing insecure, fear thoughts, to secure, safe thoughts.

It is a sure bet you will not convince yourself by changing an "I can't" thought, just once. Keep at it. Each time the thought returns, replace the "I can't," with "I can." It is really not that you can't. It is simply that you do not want to face the uncomfortable feelings and sensations which may accompany the activity.

It is common for people to gain the knowledge offered through Recovery, Inc., but to stop short. They do enough to take the edge off their symptoms. No matter how restrictive their lives are, they have created a safe space and rarely venture out of it. There is one reason only. They are scared.

People who are stuck in their own prisons of fear truly admire the progress of others. They see that they could have a brighter future, too. Unfortunately, they see the light and close their eyes. They know what to expect in their own reality and are frightened at the possibility of getting well. Consciously or unconsciously, they made the decision to "just get by."

As a group leader, at times I feel frustrated and sad when I see these individuals: sad, because I truly want them to benefit and grow as much as I have; frustrated, because information is all I can really furnish. I offer hope, but they have to accept it. I share my belief that the Recovery, Inc.

program can truly make more of an impact on their lives than their illness. Members must create their own belief, through their own practice. My practice, the vital ingredient of self-help, is impossible to give away, much as I want to.

I can teach by example, through how I live my life. But I cannot rescue. I have to realize these individuals are on their own path and not ready. I sincerely hope someday they will find their way.

I experienced some fear of getting well. I wanted to get back to work and a productive life, but I didn't know if I could handle it. After all, I was working when I had my "breakdown." I questioned whether I would be able to handle the stress and tension of a full-time position.

If you are afraid of stepping out, don't think of the world beyond as a endless abyss ready to consume you. You will learn to handle any challenge that might come along, when you learn to handle what you feel inside.

My first lesson in the process of eliminating temper (fear and anger) was to look at the irritations, frustrations and disappointments in my everyday life as trivialities instead of emergencies. Believe me, a leaf falling from a tree was about the only thing I could view as trivial. Anything that happened which even indirectly involved me was significant and serious.

Why the focus on ordinary everyday stuff? To put it very simply, there are more little irritating life lessons than there are big ones. The major events such as loss of a job, death of a loved one, divorce and serious physical illness do not occur on a daily basis.

You cannot turn knowledge into skill when you work at a task every now and then. If you are going to become good at anything, whether it is word-processing or taping drywall, you have to do it more than once a year.

If you truly want to affect a shift in your attitude, make a difference in your personal outlook on life, you can start by changing your perception of the events in your surrounding environment. The expression "don't sweat the small stuff" has been around for ages. The only way I mastered the true meaning of "small stuff," the trivialities, was by attending meetings every week and listening to people who were experts at making the differentiation.

One of the very first examples I witnessed was given by a man who told about a "triviality" which involved a bank statement he received in the morning mail. It was missing one of his deposits and he was upset. I could see being upset was certainly an average original, first response. But a triviality? No, no, no! All I could think was, "That's no triviality. A mistake that has to do with money? These people sure have a different view of reality than I do." But again, they were more calm and more emotionally stable than me, so perhaps I should try to hear, rather than merely listen. The subject of money is a *strong link*. It is likely to cause responses and after-effects in many individuals.

As I listened to the man's "spotting" and the comments from the rest of the group, I began to understand why everyone else viewed the event as a triviality. They viewed the entire incident in a *realistic*, solid, factual manner: Banks ought to track deposits correctly—true statement. People make mistakes (at banks and in every other kind of business)—also a true statement, true and rational.

The fact that he was not the first and only person to ever find an error on a statement made it average. Spotting the averageness of a situation reduces it to a triviality; takes the "poor me, why do I have to face this," and the emergency out of it. He saw the situation was distressing, but not dangerous. It was a nuisance and a hassle, not the end of the world. He would be able to handle the problem and get it corrected. He could trust his basic functions to carry him through. He would be able to call the bank or drive there. Often times, people with nervous problems think they are incapable of handling common dilemmas. We learn to *plan, decide and act*, without fear and anger.

The group also spotted that the situation was an *expectation and disappointment*. Disappointments too, are part of every day life. They can and do occur countless times throughout the day. As much as we know the world is less than perfect, we still expect life to be ideal. We live in an imperfect world. There are going to be incidents that upset us. Yet, most of us believe we should somehow be immune to them.

One of the first steps in becoming a realist is to change your attitude. The transformation can only take place when you begin to change your thoughts. The only sure way to reduce your reaction to any irritating event, to look at it as a triviality, is to view its effects in relation to your sense of inner peace. I learned to view events as trivialities only after I started using the word "triviality" in my thinking vocabulary. I cemented the lesson with these words: "*This is a triviality compared to my mental health.*" With that one phrase, making the distinction is easy. As a realist, NOTHING outweighs the importance of my mental health. It comes first, foremost and always. Because this mind-set consistently wins out, I am a winner in life.

Compare the significance of what is happening around you to the importance of the peace you are striving to attain. Consider anything and everything that upsets you from the perspective that your inner harmony is of prime importance. When you do, you will be on the path to becoming a calm, strong and centered realist.

I used to unsettle myself with what people thought about me; what they said about me or to me; what they might say about me; how they looked at me; or why they did not look at me. I always looked at the things around me with a pair of magnifying glasses, alert for negative aspects, even when they weren't truly there. It was a habit.

I thought that whatever was making me uncomfortable had to be fixed immediately, right now, on the spot. In that way, I made everything an emergency. The only thing my sense of urgency accomplished was to keep my anxiety level high.

All of us who are living, breathing, participants in life exercise three patterns of thought. We are realists, romantic thinkers and intellectuals. When the philosophies are kept in healthy balance, the realist in us regulates our thinking and behavior. We have hopes, dreams and goals. We acquire knowledge and use it wisely. We recognize what we can change and make valuable contributions to our little space in the world and to society as a whole. We live life to the fullest because we are realists.

Many people who walk the earth, especially those with nervous/mental health challenges, have a tendency to lean away from looking at life in a realistic manner.

Many people have firm convictions about everything and they want you to know them. You know the opinionated type: the person who doesn't have enough bumper for all his little stickers. (Please note that is an illustration not a judgement.) The intellectualist knows about all subjects, from taking out the trash, to choice vacation spots, to the best candidate for political office. They know there is a better way, a right and wrong to everything.

I know! I was one who had to work on judging, comparing and pointing out mistakes, my own and those of others. I may not have expressed those opinions, but they existed in my mind. Everyone I have ever met in the program admits to having had to work on achieving a healthy balance in this area. Even we are surprised at our remarkable transitions from being rigid thinkers, to being less caught up in biases.

If you purchase a "previously owned" car, and the intellectualist type notices, he may comment on it. Then he turns the conversation around to point out how the government makes a killing every time a vehicle changes owners; how unfair it is to repeatedly collect taxes on the same merchandise; how title and license tag fees, and dealer prep charges are exorbitant. The "I know" person makes statements about foreign cars sales and how they ruin the economy. Given the chance, this type personality will discuss the pros and cons of unions, how bureaucracy influences the laws, how things would be different if state or federal governments had more or less control. You will walk away wondering how the conversation turned from a new car to a lesson on the ills of the world.

When the romanticist comments on your new acquisition, he might comment favorably on it. But he will not refrain from telling you he could have made a better deal dollar-wise; he would never buy that particular make or model; or the color may not be good for re-sale and the tires will have to be replaced soon. This "I know better" person will include at least one horror story about when either he or someone he knows bought a used car. His spontaneous actions are based more on instinctive feelings than the facts. When you walk away from this lecture, you are likely to think you made an unwise purchase and question your choice, or you will be defending your decision in your own mind.

A person grounded in reality, the realist, knows the facts. The realist knows that taxes and paying some extra charges on goods and services are part of life. He may make a single passing comment on it, but not a dissertation. If asked, the realist might offer an opinion on the condition of the tires or point out something that may be a hazard. He knows that the popularity of makes, models and colors change all the time and who knows what the trend will be when and if you ever decide to sell. Those details don't matter in the present.

In the incident from the previous chapter regarding the incorrect bank statement, an intellectual believes everything should be ultimately right. There is no margin for error. The romantic thinks his own complaints and suggestions will eventually solve all the dilemmas encountered in the entire bank system. His recommendations will result in eliminating any future mistakes.

Intellectual and romantic thinkers think they know more and know better. They tend to be more subjective than objective, and act on their feelings and thoughts. The realist looks at the facts, handles the circumstance, goes on with life with a minimum of fuss. The realist knows in the end, life's irritations and frustrations are not worth getting agitated over.

Before Recovery, Inc., I was the perfect picture of what Dr.Low labeled a *romanto-intellectualist*. I lived in a world of hopes, dreams and fantasies, rather than reality. To compensate for my inner sense of insecurity, I acted inwardly and often outwardly, as if I knew more and knew better. In my mind there was a clear cut right and wrong to most things. Like all other perfectionists, I was *striving to be exceptional and feared that I was not even average*. I constantly tried to prove I was superior, to myself and to others, because I had no self-worth. I didn't believe that I was as good as the next person.

I was the fixer, the caretaker, the victim with no sense of inner self-esteem. My self-worth was attached to my outer environment, to all the things outside of me—my job, my house, my car, my friends, a significant other. Before the onset of my illness, I was a take-charge person who gave and gave to others. In return, I expected everything around me to validate me as a successful person. When circumstances changed, as they will, I felt lost and agitated, disrupted and empty.

Some of my first steps in healthy, realistic thinking were directed at improving the negative views I had of myself. If the realist inside me made a decision, the intellectualist challenged it. This personal second-guesser of mine was finally tackled with the phrase: there is no right or wrong in the trivialities of every day life. As long as I did nothing morally or ethically incorrect, I was not wrong. With plenty of practice I was able to quiet the inner voice that constantly judged me.

I no longer suffered the grave physical effects from my thinking, but I did not feel comfortable, pleasant or whole on the inside. My inner environment wasn't quite settled. I finally became sick and tired of living in a negative plane, even though it only showed on the outside as being quiet or reserved. I made a conscious decision to look for the positives in life. I did not like my negative, pessimistic thoughts, so I began to change them.

People with low self-confidence are never quite sure they have said or done the right thing in any given situation. They berate themselves for not speaking, doing or acting in just the "right" way. They review an event and think they "should" have done something differently. It can be anything as small as a conversation or as significant as a visit with the president. When you find yourself thinking, "If only I would have...," you are judging yourself wrong.

Before any situation, people with low self-esteem preview even the slightest decision and struggle making up their minds on what could or should be done. As a person with extremely high standards, I had to cultivate the *courage to make mistakes* when it came to the trivial, less important aspects in life. It wasn't that I needed to make mistakes. I had to give myself permission to make them. I had to develop an attitude of determination and trust in myself.

Many times I found I couldn't concentrate on the task at hand because I was caught up, obsessing about something that already had happened or something I was anticipating. Whether it involved the past or present, I did not view it in a positive way. If it was the past, I wished I could change it. If it was in the future, I wanted it to turn out perfectly. The truth is, the only way to create a new life is to cling to the present.

Reviewing choices when you are making decisions is healthy. Not being able to make up your mind in everyday matters keeps you tense. You will live in a constant state of stress and inevitably symptoms. It was quite a revelation to find out I created and maintained tenseness every time I put off a decision while bouncing between several alternatives.

If you think you never have trouble making up your mind, think of a time you visited a restaurant and scrutinized the lunch menu. Time to eat, but you are not sure what you want to order. Unless you made an uncompromising decision before you arrived at your destination, you are apt to mull over the menu and ask the waiter for a few more minutes to decide. If it is a fast-food place, perhaps you even let a few people go ahead of you in line while you try to make up your mind. You wrestle with yourself: tasty, cholesterol-rich bacon cheeseburger with fries or grilled chicken? Pasta or salad? Do you review your calorie intake for the last 24 hours to help make your decision or do you allow your taste buds to win? Do you settle on what someone else is ordering because you have no idea what you want?

Going to the store for a certain item and finding they are out of your favorite brand will also prompt you into facing choices. If it is not in your schedule to chase around town, do you immediately grab a similar item from the next shelf or stand and ponder a few minutes? Do you become tense and frustrated as you read the list of ingredients and try to determine if the product is as good as your preferred brand? Do you check the shelf label for price-per-weight, then start to compare and find the one shelf label lists ounces, another pounds? Do you feel like screaming because they don't make it easy to be a wise consumer? Perhaps this is why shoppers are not always in the best of moods.

Shopping for someone else is even more unnerving. Again, unless you have a specific gift item in mind and it is in stock, the choices can seem endless. The more you look and reject, the more puzzled and stressed you become. Decisions become more difficult when they involve more money and more people (unless you have total disregard for the value of your dollars or your relationships). You are not going to be as carefree when you buy a car as when you buy a loaf of bread.

All these illustrations point out hesitation, or back and forth thinking—with two intentions: to buy, or not to buy. When you have a vague or obvious fear of making a mistake, you will feel anxious and tense until you make up your mind.

The apprehension involved in making a wrong choice definitely falls into the category of a more subtle fear. If you do not work at consciously recognizing it, you will remain confused and uncomfortable. You do not simply grow out of any fear, it takes awareness and effort.

Simple everyday decisions are tough when we're under stress. The constant uncertainty and apprehension cause confusion and wreak internal havoc on our bodies and minds. There is only one solution: make a decision. A *firm decision steadies you*. Even if your decision is to put off a decision to a later date, it will calm you down. Sometimes things can wait until you obtain more information, or give your mind a rest.

What do you say to your inner voice when it starts to criticize you? What do you say to yourself when your self-confidence and self-esteem need a boost? For years now I have used this formula. When I have the original response of fear, "You blew it Rose" and follow it with a litany of "should haves" (insecure thinking) in my after-effect, I turn it around by telling myself that there is no right or wrong in the situation. I am not wrong. I am average. God knows I am not the first and only person on earth who thinks she has made a mistake in this area. And what real harm has it done? Is anyone mortally wounded or incapacitated because of my words or actions?

When you think you are wrong, be gentle with yourself by excusing yourself. Repeat the phrase, "I am not wrong, I am average," a few times and feel its magical effects.

I finally accepted being average. I figured out that being average is not "less than good," or "below par." Average is not at the top or bottom, but someplace in the middle. I am talented in some areas, maybe not in others. Some people have more formal education, some less; some are more articulate, some less. I have some shortcomings, some abilities, like millions of other souls. I am an average human being. I fit somewhere between the two extremes of inferior and superior. When I realized I was not better or worse than the majority of people who walk the earth, I stopped trying to be perfect. Today, I recognize who I am and appreciate my uniqueness. I am average, not perfect. And that is acceptable to me. It is pleasant and comfortable to be in a world without better and best, big and small, inferior and superior.

What made me stop fighting the concept of averageness? The phrase, *lower your standards and your performance will rise*. A paradox. Until I knew the true meaning, it was as complex as, "Everything is happening just the way it should, but you have a free will."

Relaxing your standards will not make you irresponsible, undependable, reckless, thoughtless or inconsiderate (as I once believed.) Ease the pressure you are putting on yourself by dropping your high expectations a notch or two. The statements reads, "lower" your standards, not drop them completely.

Believe me, if you have had all the qualities of a perfectionist all your life, lowering your standards a little isn't going to catapult you to rock bottom. You are not going to turn into a derelict or a slob. The socks in your dresser drawer and the clothing in your closet will still be arranged neatly. You will still balance your checkbook to the penny every month. You will be on time for appointments. You will still have a nice house and yard. You will not, however, be fanatic about everything around you. You will still be conscientious, considerate, reliable and respectable. Maybe even more warm and loving in their deeper meanings. Your obsessive qualities will turn into healthy ones.

If you resist the notion of softening your standards, know this fact: the sooner you learn to quit concentrating on what a perfect job you think you have to do, whatever the feat is, you will accomplish it. Instead of struggle, frustration and feeling uptight, there will be a flow. Your energy will stream forward in a smooth fashion, through the task at hand, instead of being diverted away to other channels. You will reach deadlines and goals more comfortably, with more inner peace and calm.

This is true no matter what you are trying to accomplish, from cooking a meal, to washing the car, to taking an exam. Lower your standards. Learn to set realistic goals and you will boost your productivity and performance. Convert your worry energy to problem-solving energy. Stop harassing yourself with goals that are not feasible.

In one chapter of *Mental Health Through Will Training*, Dr. Low describes a housewife who is multi-tasking, trying to do several things at once. She has started several chores, flits around from one to another. Then she begins to feel confused and overwhelmed, as if she is up against a brick wall. Trying to accomplish everything at one time is another form of having high standards.

With today's technology, it is not unusual to have several tasks going on at the same time. It is common to talk on one phone line, fax through another, while your computer operates multiple programs. The same holds true with household duties. You may have a load of clothes in the washer, one in the dryer. Dinner is in the oven and it looks like rain so you decide to mow the lawn before it starts pouring. When you spend entire days jumping from task to task, it is clear why you feel stressed and exhausted.

With the right internal components, computers can efficiently handle simultaneous tasks. As a human, you are in charge of how many jobs you choose to perform at a time. It is typical to feel as if you are running in circles when you are faced with an overload of responsibilities. But remember, if your body is in rush mode, it is impossible to feel calm, relaxed and peaceful in your mind and in your heart.

If you can multi-task without any ill-effects, wonderful. And you may be able to for a time, before it starts to wear you down. But if you find yourself feeling anxious, lower your expectations for what needs to be done. Believe me, you will feel more calm inside. Practice slowing down once in a while. Do one chore until it is complete, then go on to the next. You will be amazed at how much more calm you feel.

Recovery, Inc. does an excellent job of helping to detect other fears that hold us back. One of the majors that most of us experience is the fear of social reputation. "What do other people think of me?" I could write a series of books on my experiences with that fear alone. That solitary fear, unaccompanied by any others, will keep you locked in a prison of self-consciousness. How do you counteract it? For starters, know that in reality, most other people do not pay as close attention to you as you think. They are too busy with their own lives. They haven't the time, energy, or even the inclination to keep a close watch on you.

Since I have years of practice in this area, I have become my own person. I simply do not base my self-worth on what other people think of me. I am comfortable with who I am and my personal choices.

A few years ago I had an acquaintance who was appalled that I don't decorate my home for the Christmas holidays. At the end of a brief discussion on the subject, this person (whom I found based much of his life keeping up the appearance of being very proper) used the line, "But what will your neighbors think if you don't even have a wreath on your door?" The insecure, former Rose would have gone out and purchased some kind of outdoor decoration because someone else said it was correct (right). I still smile at what I thought in response to his comment: I have never heard of any neighborhood "wreath police" patrolling my subdivision, writing citations for naked doors. Rather than reacting insecurely with fear, I had a slightly amusing and very common-sense (realistic) thought.

Recovery, Inc. teaches *humor is our best friend, and temper is our worst enemy*. Individuals who are serious-natured, as many nervous patients tend to be, find it difficult to find any humor in life. No doubt about it, there was no amusement and enjoyment in my life for a long period of time.

Cultivating a sense of humor does not call for learning a set of one-liners so you can be witty or uproariously funny. The goal is to reframe your pessimistic attitude toward life, not to be a stand-up comic. If you are a sober, solemn type and want to break loose of the habit, step back and look at a situation as a pure observer. If it helps, picture an event that upset you as if it happened to someone else. Put another person in the starring role. Be a spectator, not a participant in the process.

Fostering a sense of humor only comes slowly and only after dropping judgement. For me, it was one of the most difficult lessons. For a long time I refused to let my guard down. The perfectionist in me kept insisting if I wasn't serious, I would be careless, when in reality, developing a light-hearted attitude only implies you are free of the burdens of the guilt, fear and anger.

When people relate the "what happened" part of their example with a smile on their face, however slight, the rest of the group can tell they are not taking themselves or the situations they find themselves in, quite as seriously as they once did. The meaning of the word "triviality" is getting through to them. They are working the Method, and it is working for them. A small grin is a clear sign of progress, the symbol of a shift in attitude. I love to see those smiles. To me, they are the outer expression of inner-healing.

25. *Release The Tension, Not The Reaction*

Along with learning to focus on "me" not being wrong, I gained valuable insight on how much scorekeeping I did with all that was going on around me. I mentioned earlier, the tools to eliminate anger and fear are almost identical. There is only one word of one phrase that is different. The phrase, "there is no right or wrong in the trivial events in life," also applies to judging other people's behavior. Knowing you are angry at someone, having the awareness and understanding, will not magically create peace and harmony in your heart. It will not relieve any physical or mental discomfort you experience. You have to go one step farther.

When I am accusing, I am the one who is suffering. Just as I learned to say, "I am not wrong" for when I judged myself, I also learned to tell myself, that other people are not wrong either. Rather than judge others, I learned to *excuse, rather than accuse.* I do not debate with wordy questions: "Is it so wrong that I am going to continue to upset my inner balance and peace? Is the situation worth making myself sick over?" I use the concise phrase: I need to excuse rather than accuse. If you only acknowledge or spot you are angry, you will stay angry. You have to offset the anger by telling yourself that the other person is not wrong, he is average.

"People are not wrong." Trust me, you are going to have trouble accepting that fact. No right or wrong? How can it be? We spend lifetimes learning the difference. When I first tried to adopt this Recovery, Inc. philosophy on an intellectual level, I was confused. All the facets of my education (and most likely yours too), whether they were parental, academic or religious, pounded the idea of right and wrong into my brain. Here I was facing pain and unrest and the Recovery, Inc. program suggested that I unlearn it all!

Yes, there are judicial system rights and wrongs, moral and ethical issues. Those are not what Recovery, Inc. philosophy address. Its' agenda centers on the stress "WE" cause ourselves when we respond to outside irritating and frustrating events. *It is not people, or places, or things, that give us our symptoms—it is our attitude towards them.* It is easy to blame someone, or something else. The reality is: people, places and things outside of us, cannot control us. They cannot make us cry, become upset, mad, sad, crazy, unhappy or depressed. We do it to ourselves.

What do I know that keeps my stress level near zero? The reality that there is no right or wrong, only differences of opinion. The fact that someone's else's opinion does not match mine, is a triviality compared to my inner peace. I still have beliefs and truths that I hold close, but I don't need to convince anyone to my way of thinking. I would never make a good politician.

I have opinions on what to wear, how to decorate my home and what flavor frozen yogurt I like best, but I can *not* afford to have opinions on who is right and who is wrong. I am well aware of the damage it does to my body, mind and spirit. I don't become infuriated about anything now, but that doesn't mean I don't have strong opinions on certain subjects. I am still passionate about mental health issues.

Responses of anger and fear are closely related. The first or original response always contains a judgement —someone is wrong. If it is not me, it must be them. If it is not them, it must be me. Attitude is formed during after-effect. It is the thoughts, at this point, that fuel how you feel and where things are apt to be blown out of proportion. And there is only one way to change your attitude—change your thinking.

There is great power and danger in your thoughts. Learn to listen to them. They can jeopardize your health or enhance it. When you think someone is wrong, replace the thought with, "he is not wrong he is average." When you think you are wrong, change the thought to, "I am not wrong, I am average." This is the only valid way to neutralize your temper, eradicate mind/body discomforts, and gain peace and harmony. The more you try to control your outer environment, the more "out of control" you will feel on the inside, in your inner environment.

We are taught to think in opposites, right/wrong, up/down, hot/cold. It is natural to think if I say someone isn't wrong, he must be right. Not so. The sole purpose of ruling someone not wrong is to put a stop to the vicious cycle of anger. Telling myself someone is not wrong allows me to step off my subconscious treadmill and put a stop to the internal commotion I've created. In very simple terms, run-on anger makes me sick every time I indulge in it.

Anger robs peace, and produces unpleasant side-affects. This is a concept which does not become a truth overnight. At first, I only used the words, "he is Not wrong," because the program advocated them. When someone did something I interpreted as wrong, I repeated either, "he is not wrong, he is average," or "she is not wrong, she is average." It was purely mechanical. When you realize your mental health is involved, you will do anything. It is a survival instinct. Sometimes I thought the phrase. Many times I would recite it out loud. Sometimes I still do. For example, when I am trying to calm myself after someone cuts me off in traffic.

There are times when I am obligated to listen to someone I disagree with completely. When I find my internal peace fading because I am judging myself right and the other person wrong, I take time to calm down my internal environment. It may seem as if I am giving the person my undivided attention, when in fact in my mind I am repeating, "she is not wrong, she is average," or "he is not wrong, he is average."

Many years ago I added a tune to the anger-neutralizing phrase and made it sound like a little rhyme. More than one person at a Recovery, Inc. meeting has heard it. This is one of the ways I discovered to add humor to a sometimes dull process. Practicing these methods can get boring. I tried to add variety to "how" I did it, not deviating from the basic "what" needed to be worked on. I am sure many others have done the same.

I learned that acting on angry thoughts only promotes retaliation. If you try to tell people they are wrong, they are going to try to prove themselves right. Your tension will only escalate and produce a larger variety or more severe symptoms. Instead of a queasy stomach, you will have a pain in your gut. You will exchange a small headache, for a piercing pain in your temples. Along with the physical discomfort, you will start feeling confused.

You can be *pre-disposed to temper*. Looking at or thinking about certain people triggers the memory of something they have done, and you can go into the working-up process. I have mentally tattooed a bright red "OE" (for Outer Environment) on many a person's forehead. It was my reminder I had no control over them, and a cue for me to control my speech muscles and not initiate a discussion which would very likely instigate a heated exchange.

Even when I feel people are impolite and inconsiderate, insulting, rude or offensive, according to my standards or those of society, I spot to myself: they are not wrong, they are average. *Outer environment can be rude, crude and indifferent*. There are always going to be those who act in a less-than-considerate manner. Whether the behavior is directed at me or I am a bystander, it is a trivial incident when I equate it with my inner peace.

I still don't appreciate it when a hotel desk clerk doesn't smile once at any time during the check-in process. I still notice, I am human. In fact, I think all persons, in any service occupation should go to "smile school." But I also know genuine smiles come from inside, from feeling good about yourself. And, I do encounter plenty of authentic smiles wherever I go.

When you excuse someone else, you are NOT condoning their inappropriate actions. You are letting go of what is making you upset. Sometimes you do have to release someone else's unacceptable behavior, for your own mental well-being. The negative words and crass behavior of others provoke original responses of hurt and anger. But, it is your negative thinking, the anger and fear processed in an after-effect, which hurt you even more.

No one enjoys being treated in a less than caring way, or being on the receiving end of an abusive verbal assault. It is normal and average to have a response, even a strong one. The after-effect which follows is full of: "How could he or she have..., I just don't understand..." These thoughts frequently keep an after-effect thrashing through your mind for hours or days. Often longer. When my angry thoughts whirl out of control, I say to myself, "he is not wrong, he is average." Invariably the next thoughts run along the lines of "But I expect...; But I deserve...; But I would never do that; But he *is* wrong."

Every "but..." thought keeps a vicious cycle alive and manifests symptoms. And every "but..." has to be counteracted with another "he is not wrong, he is average." I finally put a big mental exclamation point after, "he is not wrong, he is average!" For me, it creates a solid definitive end. It is my stop sign to keep the whispers of angry thinking from returning.

You can reject the truth of "no right or wrong," or debate it. Or, you can make use of it to reduce your stress and perhaps eventually accept the fact. You can dilute the words by saying: "She didn't know what she was doing" or " He really didn't mean it." Or think, "They are only acting as they know how." But, why bother. Attack your anger at the core, stop judging right and wrong. Don't you wish there were little alarm lights to alert you when you are judging someone? There are—the negative body and mind sensations you experience and label as stress.

I also found it helpful to repeat this anger-neutralizing phrase several times in a row, not necessarily rapidly, but methodically. At times I picture the words in my mind as if they were on a TelePrompTer. When I repeat the excusing thought, it simply doesn't leave time or room for the angry thoughts. It does calm me down. Feeling calm and being in control of myself are my ultimate goals.

Recovery, Inc. helped me recognize a typical temper situation that I call third-party anger. It is easy to become a player in this game. It happens when I become angry at someone who has done something that upset someone I care about. I do not have to witness the incident, only hear about it to become entangled in my own after-effect.

You have been through it. Your sister calls and tells you what your mother did or said to her while they were shopping. Bang! You are in after-effect. You try to figure out who was wrong. Perhaps a co-worker tells you about someone she had a discussion with. At first you listen. As she goes on, you find yourself forming opinions, taking sides as to who is right.

I have even experienced the, "I don't even know you, and I am miffed at you" anger. Think that it never happened to you? Read on. Your friend calls and tells you about the "snide" remark his manager made to him. Or he goes on about how unfairly he is being treated. You have never met his supervisor, never even been near his workplace, but you get caught up in judging right and wrong. "How could they treat him that way?"

If you are level-headed enough to try to be the mediator, there is a good chance the person is not looking for advice, but sympathy. He is looking for someone to verify that he is "right." If he is looking for support and guidance, it is your choice to offer it. Be aware, not everyone will be open-minded and listen.

The anger we direct at others is often a result of not understanding the person's actions or behavior. You will *never* completely understand the motives behind someone else's behavior. So don't even try. It will only keep your tension level high. Half of the time you don't comprehend your own actions. You simply do what you do. What makes you think you would be any better at figuring out someone else?

I used to play the game of amateur therapist and try to psychoanalyze. How many of you live with the common misconception if we love or like a person, we have to understand? It is not true, and does not only pertain to life-partner love. It extends to all human relationships. There is only one outcome from repeatedly questioning the actions of others. You stay in a state of upheaval while the other person keeps acting in the manner he chooses or in the only way he knows how. He goes on living, and you continue to suffer.

Until you can make the statement, "I don't understand and I don't have to," you are still considering the other person wrong. If you were judging him right, you wouldn't be embroiled in trying to figure out his behavior.

We do not sit around and process the reason people do pleasant things for us, do we? You have never spent a whole day thinking about why the cashier at the drug store was cordial to you. She was right. Yet, you dwell on the person who you believe was abrupt to you and believe he was wrong. You carry around that unpleasant person in your mind as long as you choose to judge.

If you find yourself furious and thinking a certain someone is *"always"* inconsiderate, or "never" does her share, you already know those individuals are acting their own way. Using the word *"always,"* indicates you have witnessed the behavior before. That it is standard operating conduct for the individual. It is their average. Look at it rationally. What else do you expect from them if they are acting the way they always act? A miracle transformation? An overnight conversion? Their habits may not be what you would like to see or hear. It is however, how they behave. It is their average.

You can say, "I know, but I wish..." for the rest of your life, and people may never change. You don't like how they act, and you don't have to. What is important to realize is this: <u>the longer you stay angry, annoyed, enraged or irritated, the more you affect your health</u>.

Watch the extremes. Are the terms "always" and "never" accurate, or an exaggeration? Be realistic. Is it always? Most of the time? Some of the time? Be honest.

Know this truth: <u>The longer you put off cancelling the anger, the more pain you are going to experience</u>. You set the time limit. Do you want to suffer for an hour or two, or for a few days? Go ahead. Put off releasing your anger for that long. It is your choice. Either put your energy into justifying your right to be "right" and continue living your misery, or put the same energy to work and focus on dissipating the anger, and act on your right to be healthy and peaceful. If you find yourself agitated the minute you awaken, check for your unresolved anger.

"Excuse rather than accuse." Another tidy four word statement for your resource pool, to keep your showers from turning into storms.

I can assure you, this formula of excusing the people you have no real control over anyway will not turn you into a wimp. It will not make you ineffective in dealing with others. You may no longer outwardly dominate, but you will know, without a doubt, that you are in control of every situation you have to face. Today, I allow less unacceptable behavior in my life than ever before. My self-respect is firmly ingrained. And I give it away to no one.

In the after-effect of an angry response, we think about how we can "right" a situation. And, as much as we hate to admit it, we have some thoughts about how we can get even. We want to prove the other person(s) wrong and ourselves right.

No, it is not good for you to keep anger bottled up inside, but it is just as dangerous to go into a rage and explode. No one disputes that you have a right to your opinion. The program does not foster your turning into a doormat for people to walk all over. It teaches us to: *express your feelings and suppress your temper*. In my mind that is an art.

When you speak and express your feelings in an even-tempered manner, you feel a sense of relief. Unless you have had a lot of experience, it will take a long time before you can express how you feel with even the barest amount of charm, grace, dignity and class. You will stammer through the learning process just as the rest of us staggered through it. So what if your words don't come out right the first time? At least you have made a start. Remember, you don't need to be eloquent, only effective. Resolve your anger inside, before you express your thoughts to others.

When you express anger by being irritable or flying off the handle, sometime in the future you will not feel good about what you did. You will judge yourself wrong for the way you acted, and very likely never admit it to another soul. Recovery, Inc. calls these, *symbolic or shallow victories*. The temporary feeling of power, feeling alive and in charge, does not last. When you rant, rave, rage, roar or go on a rampage, you are not expressing your emotions, you are displaying emotional behavior. You are acting out of control. That is why you will berate yourself afterwards. A counterattack is not justifiable. Make your victories healthy ones, over your temper—not the people around you.

Recovery, Inc. techniques teach those people who can't speak up, to communicate and be assertive. They teach people who are domineering to communicate and be assertive, without being overpowering. There is a method for everyone.

When I find myself in a volatile, unstable or emotional situation, I tell myself: *calm begets calm*. If I work at remaining calm and in control, chances are I will stay that way. If I have the opportunity, I physically remove myself from the place of conflict, and take a *cooling-off period*. If I can't leave, I close my mind off for a few seconds and do something not quite so noticeable, glance out a window or in another direction. When I use the Recovery, Inc. dictum, *turn a cool and chilly shoulder toward the situation*, I do a mental about-face. In my mind, I see myself turning around and ignoring what is going on.

On occasion, when my *goal is peace in my inner environment, I might see the bonus of peace in the outer environment*. If I don't add anger and negative energy to a situation, what is happening around me may be less stormy. This isn't always the case. The added bonus isn't always a reality. To me, however, it *is* worth the effort. Because the process consistently nourishes *my* inner peace.

No matter what uncomfortable situation I find myself in, I know it is **phasic and not basic**. It is not going to last forever. Many life situations are uncomfortable. That is reality. Taking exams or having an auditor at your side for a few days reviewing your performance can be unnerving. So can a host of other things. You know what they are in your life, the "I hate it when ..." things. Even the first time you attempt *anything* it can be uncomfortable. *You cannot be comfortable in an uncomfortable situation*. But know that situation will not last forever.

Sometimes I find that I have the *choice of two discomforts*. Either I can brave what has to be faced and be uncomfortable. Or, I can procrastinate and suffer through the discomfort I create when I go through mentally kicking myself for not facing my fear.

There are other Recovery, Inc. spotting slogans which were mentioned in previous chapters on symptom-management that fit when you find yourself tied up in anger or fear. Start by putting things in perspective—the situation is a triviality compared to your mental well-being.

Change your thoughts. Replace insecure thoughts with secure thoughts. It is similar to using the search/replace function of your word processing program. When you are angry, you feel threatened and unsafe because you are unable to control what is going on inside you and around you. Make yourself feel safe with the core secure thought, "This is distressing, but not dangerous." It may be upsetting, very upsetting (distressing), but it's not dangerous. You will be able to take care of yourself. Repeat: "There is no danger, there is no danger."

In my mind, and this is above and beyond Recovery, Inc. standards, if a situation is not life-threatening to me or to others, I see it as a triviality, not a crisis. I am positive this view is not shared by everyone who has gone through the program, but it works for me. I do not fear events, present or future. Because my mind is no longer muddled with temper (fear or anger), I think and act in a rational manner. I have no trouble deciding where the line exists between what is a triviality and what is a non-triviality.

Believe me, that is half the battle. I see people struggle with it all the time. Labeling something a triviality does not mean that it is completely unimportant. It means that you are not willing to make yourself sick over it. Set *your* own standard for what is trivial compared to your mental health, then live by it.

If I run into something I cannot handle on my own, I see someone who is more knowledgeable than I am on the subject. A few months after my mother's death I decided to talk to a ministerial counselor about grief. I was in new territory. I had never lost a parent before and needed some guidance for what I was experiencing. When I sell or buy a house, I employ the best real estate agent and attorney I know. When I have a medical matter, I go to the best physician I know. If they do not furnish the services satisfactorily, I choose other specialists. There is an entire world of resources out there. I use them.

There are things in life which are out of the realm of self-help. In the Recovery, Inc. program, we are encouraged to be wise and seek outside assistance. Having self-help skills gives you an edge on what goes on in life. It also makes you sensible enough to know when to seek an expert.

Wants versus needs, the "must have's" and "nice to have's," also come into play in dealing with anger. When I want to tell someone just what I think, I have to weigh what I want against what I really need. Above everything in the universe, what do I need most? My mental well-being. Choose *your* most important need, then live by it.

If you neutralize your temper as soon as possible, it will dissipate, and you won't reach the blow-out point. Work at keeping each irritation, frustration and disappointment separate and minor. Manage your days, one response at a time. Trust me, it is easier. Handling each triviality as it comes along is a process, a business. But then, so is life.

When I want to tell someone just what I think, I can

command my speech muscles to keep quiet. I can control the impulse, if I take a moment to make the choice. Every act of self-control, produces a sense of self-respect. I will like myself better in the end because I showed some control. Another advantage is an increase in my self-confidence. I know I posses the internal power to regulate my behavior. If I am in a situation which requires me to do something, I try not to speak or act in a coarse manner. I call on the actress in me to be polite and considerate, maybe even gracious. Even when I don't feel that way inside. It is like wearing a mask—*not giving outer expression to inner feelings.* I remember that an *insincere gesture of friendliness, is more beneficial than a sincere gesture of hostility.*

An insincere gesture is not hypocritical or fake, it is civil. It means treating people with respect, even when you question whether they deserve that respect. It is a sincere act of being not-so-sincere. It is one of the short-range acts which adds to my long-range goal, my genuine desire and intent to change and grow. Always remember, the respect you have for yourself is mirrored in what and how you speak to others.

The Recovery, Inc. program does not condone the expression of verbal or non-verbal anger, but also teaches that no one is perfect. There will be times when we display our displeasure. We raise our voices, slam doors, and phone receivers or stomp away from someone. After all, we are mortals, not saints. We are not going to comply with the guidelines 100% of the time. Our goal is to reduce the number of times we exhibit temper, in any way, shape or form. The more you practice, the easier it is to control the impulses. During my personal training program, it was important for me to not blame myself if I did have a strong response and react to something. *Have your temper, but don't make an issue of it.* It does not mean I could justify my anger. For my own health, I couldn't afford a new vicious cycle, one where I continued to beat myself up for making a mistake.

In Recovery, Inc. I learned practice needs to stay

consistent, but not necessarily absolute. It is not like a chemical addiction where a person has to totally abstain. I can have an impulsive flare of temper (anger or fear) every once in a while. On occasion, I have a five-minute Rose-bashing session. But it only puts me in a more rotten mood, so I give it up.

Even after I had the knowledge and was applying it and making good gains, I had a tendency to cast blame at myself, for even my first responses—all because of my ultra high standards. I did not act outwardly on the responses, but I mentally berated myself for even thinking them. "What's wrong with me? Other people are not so sensitive." I was the classic *impatient patient*. Everyone suffers from it at one time or another. You make a little progress, and you want to be totally well. You want to be rid of *all* your faulty thinking. I looked at my self-proclaimed role-models, who had been in the program for years, and expected to be like them. When I focused on my improvements, not theirs, I learned to be patient with myself. Patience is another little by-product of the program.

Being eager to make progress is not any different than anyone else being impatient in what they are trying to learn. Start anything new, piano or tennis lessons, and there is a frustration threshold you have to cross before you feel comfortable. When you are a novice or apprentice, you simply do not have the level of expertise. It is not how quickly, but the fact that you are learning and growing that is important.

We all want quick fixes when we are not feeling good. We have our tolerance levels for pain and discomfort, but when any illness lasts too long we are ready for it to depart. Have you ever been sick and tired of feeling sick and tired? Perhaps when you are at the tail end of a good bout with the flu. Anyone who has had a broken bone can tell you they "made do" with the cast for a while, then reached a point when they were ready for it to be gone! We are a society that expects to take a pill and feel better in the morning—for all that ails us.

My advice for those anxious to see more progress is to stick with the good things they are doing and continue to work hard. You do not have to do it all, right now. Look at your own "before Recovery" portrait. Be assured that, yes, I have walked in your shoes, and I made it through. Will-training seems like a lot of work, but you will see the benefits when you focus on *your* initial improvements. Don't ignore the gains, no matter how small they may seem to you. Everyone in the world can point out your progress to you, but *you* have to recognize *your* improvements. It is the *self* part of the self-help formula.

When you finally believe in yourself, you will believe in the Method. When the belief comes, so will the understanding. Doubts will fade and be replaced with a sense of accomplishment, a *realistic sense of self-pride*. You will feel your *inner smile*—joy, light and peace at an inner level.

One of the rewards of working on one irritation after another is that, after a time, you find the things that used to bother you don't anymore. You honestly reduce the number of original responses. Any Recovery person with experience can tell more than one story about something that used to drive them crazy, that doesn't even faze them anymore. Every once in a while I will find myself in a situation, such as waiting in a slow moving line at the airport check-in counter, and notice I am not having a response to the fact that it is hardly inching forward. Years ago, I would have been stressed. And more stresses would have continued to build on top of that.

Recently I gave an example at a meeting and mentioned in a somewhat serious and concerned tone of voice that I hadn't had such a strong response in a long, long while. I was surprised. I remember wondering, "Where did that (response) come from?" Someone at the group pointed out that I was interpreting insecurely. She repeated the same sentence with a different inflection in her voice and a smile, "Rose hasn't had such a strong response in a long, long while." Same sentence, totally opposite meaning. The person changed the connotation of what I was thinking, from insecure to secure with just a simple smile. It was a good reminder to me and the rest of the group, to see how simple the Method can be if we take the time to alert ourselves to what we dwell on. Look at the tone of your thoughts. They can whine just as if you spoke them. We think in words and our thoughts can contain the same inflection as our speech. I find it helpful to speak my new thinking aloud. Somehow it cements it in my brain.

Often when persons with mental health challenges have temper outbursts, it is the only time they do feel vital and in control. Hours and days of depression, anxiety and fear are a pretty drab existence. If you look around, most of our lives are routine and predictable. Day in and day out you perform the same rituals: eat, sleep, work. Weekend activities become habits too. All in all, a pretty boring existence. A little temper adds a little excitement. It starts the adrenalin pumping again and makes you feel alive and in control. I know. Even after I was in the program awhile, I had a hard time understanding why I craved temper. It wasn't until I had a taste of true peace, that I was able to discard my habit of judging right and wrong.

Anger and fear are frustrating, upsetting emotions that throw off your body's equilibrium. If you don't want to give up all your emotions, embrace the healthy, stimulating ones: respect, affection, compassion, friendship and love. They literally activate your body's energy and make positive changes in how you feel. They stimulate a healthy high.

In life we interact with other beings. We are part of a team, even though sometimes we would rather not be. Throughout my training I was reminded to be *group-minded*—to think about my behavior with regard to the people around me. If I am in the presence of at least one other person, I am part of group, and I need to consider all feelings.

Those who are the closest to us are sometimes the only ones who see our tantrums and ill-behavior. We forget their state of well-being and stress level are affected by our moods and actions (as we are by theirs). In our other life scenarios we act on our best behavior. We are often more kind to our customers than we are to our family. When in truth, it ought to be the other way around. We should be considerate in all of our human contacts, and most kind and gentle to those in our closest relationships.

Most people are uncomfortable even being innocent spectators, witnessing someone else's confrontations. Remember, the heated conversations you are involved in cause anxiety to both you and the other person.

To me, being group-minded means living life in a fashion which creates peace for me and those around me. It not only means I don't direct criticism at them, it also means that I don't come home from work and complain about every terrible thing that happened to me. Resolve conflicts of fear and anger in your own mind, and you will not expect others to do it for you. Group-minded also means being cooperative, looking at the goals of the group instead of just your own. Sometimes it means stretching out of your comfort zone for the sake of others and reaching a healthy compromise. I think of it as a balance between doing for myself and doing for others.

I never realized how swiftly I could shift my mood until it was pointed out to me. Let me illustrate. You are at home, busy raising your voice about some issue. The doorbell rings. You stomp over to the door and open it. It is your new neighbor and she wants to use your phone because her phone isn't working. You smile and invite her in. Think about it! It did not take more than a split second to change your disposition—from cranky to calm, from agitated to more tranquil. Look at the smooth transition you made in no time at all because it was your conscious intent. Because of previous programming, somewhere in your past, you have made it your habit not to show the disagreeable side of your character to the people who live next door.

After you stop and think, and pick out an event in your life when you made a similar shift, it is impossible to believe you cannot change habitual tendencies, no matter how ingrained you think they may be. You can change your behavior, if it is your intent.

We change our attitude in situations all the time. How many times have you locked your temper in your office home or car, gone on with other activities, then picked it up again when you returned? Have you ever had a disagreement with someone on the way to an event, put it on hold because other people were around and later picked up where you left off? If you haven't resolved it in your mind, you either start to talk, or are sullen and silent.

I will be very honest with you. You will have to work consistently to overpower anger and fear—the co-conspirators which rob your peace. That's consistently, not constantly. You need to maintain a steady forward pace. And, once you have some initial success in breaking the habit of overanalyzing and have gained a pretty healthy measure of stability and self-respect, then it is going to seem a nuisance to have to keep at it. You will become lazy. You will forget. And you will start feeling the effects again. Keep ignoring what you have to do to stay mentally fit, and you will go back to all your old habits and your old anxiety.

There are enough trivial, upsetting situations to fill an encyclopedia. Daily life is brimming with them—your child throws a tantrum, after you give him what he has been whining for; you have car trouble; the boss adds one more thing to today's list of to-do's, so it is time to prioritize, one more time; someone forgot to stop and pick up your prescription and now has to go back out; someone hasn't called you when she said she would; someone has called and cancelled an appointment; you have finally taken a mental health day, the weather was supposed to be sunny and it is raining, causing you to cancel the trip to the lake; the UPS driver did not deliver the package that you expected.

In addition to these events being labeled irritations and frustrations, in Recovery we are taught to view them as expectations and disappointments. If you anticipate going from point A to point B in 30 minutes and it takes you 45, that is a disappointment. If you know disappointments are simply a part of life, you will not be quite as disappointed when they come along. Another item to add to your reality training.

There are also times when we have a pre-conceived idea that things will go a certain way: you work hard at preparing a presentation, think your customer will love it and she doesn't; you go to a social event with a new partner in hopes of making your old one jealous, and former partner doesn't even notice you; you believe a call from a certain person on your birthday will make your day wonderful, and the call never comes; you tell your children to pick up their toys, they promise to "from now on," then don't. These are samples of when we receive responses because an outcome is not what was imagined. You do something, expect positive results and find it did not go as planned. *Self-appointed expectations lead to self-induced frustrations.* These self-designed disappointments are also part of a typical day.

Another kind of disappointment comes into play when we feel people don't notice or appreciate us. These are instances when we feel our *self-importance was stepped on*. It's is a little ego matter that can be solved with two techniques. Excuse the other person, and endorse yourself for your effort.

All these little events are what I label CTP's, my acronym for "chances to practice." CTP's are learning aids. Gifts (sic), not always welcome ones, that provide opportunities to use your new-found knowledge. They are the occasions to act on your commitment to growth.

Any of us can sit around and talk about how enlightened we are with new knowledge, but until we put new ideas into practice we never change or grow. Practice is the only way to truly cast aside old thinking. As in learning any new skill, it involves several attempts. It is how you develop your own *Will to effort*. When you are in training, you aim at the same goal more than once before you are successful. When that goal is finally achieved, you go on to another. The very definition of training is you are going to *try and fail, try and fail, try and succeed*.

Mr. Placekicker does not go out and boot a field

goal on Sunday afternoon without missing a few during practice sessions. A baseball player does not get a hit every time at bat. And you are not going to succeed in all of your attempts.

Don't expect to fail, but know it is okay when you do. It is going to take more than one attempt to cast aside old thinking and feelings. That is realistic. The prescribed exercises of the Recovery, Inc. Method are simple. Change your thoughts and command your muscles. That is not too complicated. But it is not always easy. If you make an attempt and feel you have not succeeded, re-affirm your goals and wait for the next chance to practice. Expect to eventually succeed and you will!

Every one of your attempts, along with the small successes, go into a pseudo bank of *past practice*. The next time you find yourself in a similar situation, you draw on the secure, safe thought that you have faced a parallel circumstance before and made it through. It works with any situation of fear and anger. You know the event is causing you to feel stressed, but you can make it through because you have in the past. You built up stamina and nerve resistance with each CTP.

You are the sole owner of your "past practice" account. No one else in the universe can contribute to it. Adding to the assets is a gradual process. Each time you work on a CTP, you add a deposit. Even when you draw on it, you never draw from it. It never reduces in size, it keeps building, getting larger and larger.

After years of practice, my bank is so solid, I truly believe there is nothing I can't accomplish. There may be things I choose not to do, but there is nothing I cannot do. There is nothing I can't face and conquer. Wouldn't you like to feel the same way? Incorporate some of the techniques in this book into your manner of living and start your own, "past practice" account.

The program teaches about *sabotage*—when you are able and prepared, but not willing, to put your knowledge into practice. Sabotage is when you know what to do, and fail to do it. Perhaps it is a case of selective amnesia. Or a conscious or unconscious idea your misfortune is making you feel special for the first time in your life, and you don't want to give it up. Once you learn WHAT to do, it is up to you and only you, to make an effort. It is time to take responsibility for your level of wellness. Do not ignore the "CTP's" (chances to practice) in your life. Use them. Sabotage only delays progress. Inner peace or inner turmoil? It is really your own choice when you have the knowledge of what to do.

My personal outline was to first target a central area or a behavior to work on, find at least one tool and use it as often as I had the chance. Because of the severity of what and how I was feeling, managing the symptoms had to come first. I had to start to function again in the outside world. Then I branched out, not ignoring my first goal, but broadening the scope of practice.

This program requires more of your time than your money. And if your comeback is, "Ah, but time IS money," my reply is, "Health IS wealth!" Most people spend more time on their possessions rather than their minds, and wonder what is wrong.

Look around at the people you know who walk around with genuine smiles on their faces and a sparkle in their eyes. There may be a few who came by their sunny disposition naturally, but I would wager the great majority had to work on it sometime during their lives. If you think you were born lacking certain happy genes, or your life circumstances have robbed you of ever feeling joy again—know that if you want, you can change. Don't give outer expression to your inner sadness; don't let it be written "all over your face." Practice those insincere gestures of friendliness until they become natural. You can command your face muscles to smile instead of looking so serious. When you do you will reap the benefits. You will feel good, and there is nothing better than feeling good.

Before Recovery, Inc. I had standards for myself and the rest of humanity only the gods could reach. Because I had nothing to help me cut into the thought processes, my other voice (the one inside) could litter my mind for days. Most times, the people, places and things I was angry at were only present in my mind. Each time I reviewed an event I relived it, because the mind doesn't know the difference between a real and an imaginary scene.

Very early in my training, I learned to stop repeating everything that happened to anyone or everyone who would listen, perhaps to many who did not want to listen. *To talk it up is to work it up.* I always wondered why I couldn't forget about negative events. It was simply because I kept them alive by talking about them, out loud or to myself.

If I had an inkling that I made a mistake, I would judge myself worthless by dredging up all my past "failures," recent and otherwise. If I processed the after-effect stage long enough, I could go back to being six years old—making the negative the focal point and totally ignoring any good memories. It was the same if I thought someone else was wrong. I would review the mental checklist I had on them. Through regular and repeated practice, I have obliterated the negative lists, mine and everyone else's.

There are life circumstances which put us in contact with people we find almost impossible to deal with. You can have a single, occasional encounter with this type person, or it may be someone you can't avoid. It could be a clerk at a gas station, a client, your employer, or someone in your family. Whoever or whenever, there are individuals that irritate you to no end. Communicating with them is aggravating. Being in their presence seems to bring out the worst in you, and in them. In these circumstances you do the best to understand and be polite, but still feel drained. It is exasperating; no matter what you do, you are not right, or it is not enough. Very often we tolerate these people to their faces, but complain about them behind their backs. Complaining is a working-up process.

In Recovery, Inc. these are called *temperamental deadlocks.* There is a stand-off, simply because you think you are right and the other person thinks he is right. You will never eliminate the deadlock completely if the other person doesn't do some changing of his or her own. You can, however, be free of some of the consistent disturbances that plague your body and mind. You can become the observer of, rather than a full participant in the temper. Once you have some practice in not judging a person wrong, for your own benefit, you will see some amazing differences. The other person will still be disagreeable and negative, but you will be more calm. You will see you that you do have control, inner control, and you will be proud of yourself. You can stop asking the question, "Why do I let her get to me?"

When you are at an impasse, ask yourself: "Do I want to be right, or do I want to be healthy?" Know that the only thing you give up is the root of your discontent.

Every day you have different ideas and different views about various things. As we process information, our realm of understanding and acceptance should naturally expand. You certainly don't have the identical view of things and the same wants as you did when you were a teenager or young adult. Be honest. There are foods you wouldn't touch before, which you enjoy now; places and activities you didn't care for, which are now included on your list of preferences.

Personal opinions and preferences are just that, personal. Yours belong to you. Mine belong to me. If they don't match, they don't match. Opinions are like noses —everyone has their own and they are all unique. The facts are, no one is going to agree with 100 percent of what you believe, 100 percent of the time, and you are not going to always conform to all their views.

Anger is intellectual blindness to the other person's point of view. I used to think I was an open-minded person. Now I know I am. There is invariably another side to every story. I know that fact, and don't even have to try and figure out what the other side might be. I know what shape I was in when I was constantly judging, and frankly I did not like it. I treasure my inner peace and I am not getting back on that emotional roller coaster.

We don't argue about genuine issues, we argue to prove we are right. Plain and simple, we do not want to be wrong. You can throw out a lot of facts, but there is only one opinion. Facts stand on their own. Right and wrong are only assumptions, opinions. When I make the statement, "I *think* I am right," I am only assuming and presuming, based on the information I have. I do not *know* without a doubt that I am right.

There is a very simple formula for stopping a dispute, debate or disagreement, one that is on your lips or in your mind, along with all the turmoil it is causing you —stop trying to prove you are right. Is your churning stomach, the tightness in your chest and the pain in your neck worth the momentary pleasure of thinking you are right? Believe me, it is not. The nasty physical feelings and mental discomforts last much longer than the one "sweet moment" you enjoy as the thrill of victory. The ultimate technique for erasing anger is to take out the right and wrong, and look at the facts.

In my world, if someone else needs to be right, it is okay with me. I can make a statement, by not making a statement. I can give up my "right" to be right, but I will not give up my "right" to be healthy.

You can bring up a lot of different issues, with lots of "But if's..." If you want to feel better, get off your "buts" and admit you are angry or fearful.

After all these pages do you still feel as if you are not in control of your life? That it is in someone else's hands—your doctor's, your employer's, your spouse, your parents', your building contractor? Has anyone tried to tell you, your future is in your hands and you don't believe it? I agree. It is not in your hands. It is in your head, in your thoughts. Your future, from this moment forward belongs to you. You are in control. You are steering. You are the pilot. Like it or not, you are in charge. Sorry, you can't pass the responsibility off to anyone else.

It is common to have your present life in good order

and start drifting back to the resentments and hurts of the past and mourn the time you think you have lost. Although it is not part of the program to do it, I was able to heal those scars in my soul and mind, forgive and forget a number of significant unresolved past issues with these same Recovery, Inc. tools: I am not the judge of who is right and wrong; people are not wrong, they are average; each and every person I have encountered is my outer environment. In fact, the past too, is outer environment, outside my inner plane. What remains are neutral, healthy memories. I have let go of the old baggage and more important, I have the devices I need to keep from creating any more.

Most of us are not in the habit of being infuriated about, or mulling over the good things that go on in life. It is always the opposite. When you find yourself perturbed, second guessing and thinking negatively about anything that was said, to or about you, stop and spot. Take a reality check. There is a very good chance you are *interpreting insecurely*. So many of us are *keen observers and poor interpreters* when it comes to life. We are adept at spying, but not so competent at picking out the real and positive. When I came into Recovery, Inc. I fit that pattern. I jumped to conclusions all the time. If I "thought" something and was unsure, I only had a suspicion. I did not know the true facts. If I thought my boss considered me incompetent because I asked a lot of questions about a new assignment, it was a suspicion, not a fact. If I thought my aunt judged me inconsiderate because I did not have time to return her phone call, it was a suspicion, not a fact. The fact that you are "not sure," is the secure thought. All you really know is—you do not know.

Let me add two realistic thoughts. In the case of the boss—he wouldn't have given me the assignment in the first place if he did not think I was capable or up to the challenge. My aunt, much as I love her, if she is angry because I did not call her this one time, then she has her own anger to take care of.

Part of the reality training the Method provides is to

look at the *total view*, rather the *partial view*. It is learning to scan the big picture instead of zeroing in on a single, negative aspect. It is a process of assessing *all* the facts, instead of only one. Looking at the total view is one of the mechanisms I use to shift into a more positive thinking mode. Ask yourself this: Why make your thoughts negative and harsh when they can be positive and kind?

Temper blocks insight. You will not see alternatives until you crumble the barrier set up by insecure, unsafe and angry thoughts. Judgement impairs ability, creates a narrow view and locks thoughts, opinions and attitudes into a narrow bumpy path. When you move out of the temper lane, you see there is smooth sailing a slight distance away. You cannot expand when you have tunnel vision. With insight you are able to make decisions based on wisdom, not emotions. With insight you learn to evaluate, instead of judge. Temper keeps captives; insight opens broader fields, to the options at hand, if you choose to take them.

Before Recovery, Inc., I was so full of angry and fearful thoughts I truly believed I had no choices in most matters. You don't have to carry a psychiatric label to feel the same. When you think or speak the words, "I haven't any choice" or feel you are being pressured and don't know what to do, look for the fear and anger you harbor. Take a tour of your mind and listen to your thoughts. After dissipating some of the temper, you will be able to think more rationally.

When I began to look at things as wants instead of needs, it broadened my scope of alternatives. When you decide you *need* something, you narrow your choices. If you "need" a pair of purple socks, nothing will do but purple. If the store doesn't have them, you are out of choices, period. But, if you "want" a pair of purple socks, and there are none, you still have other choices (another color or another store).

The reality is: there are alternatives to everything. If you have examined the options and still decide to do nothing, that is a choice in itself. Stop playing the victim, you have made a choice to not make a change. But it does not mean you are locked into the choice, that you have used up all the decisions allotted to you. You did not come into life with a preset quantity of 4,000 choices. No one is keeping track of the total but you. Life is full of opportunities and change, therefore, full of decisions.

Were we all brought up to believe decisions are written in stone, or was it just me? If you make a decision, it does not mean you cannot make a different one. If you make a new decision, it does not make the first one wrong. One decision does not necessarily mean a conclusion. There is not one optimum, defined path. You can interpret that fact securely with a smile, and know that you are free to choose. Or you can interpret the fact insecurely with a frown, and dread all the decisions that face you in the future.

26. *Run-on Fear*

Unchecked fear expands to worry—same book different title. Worry is another level of fear. It is a case of after-effect stuck in high gear, running wild. In truth, it is a preoccupation with a danger theme. We often express worry and concern (fear) to mask anger. Many of us were raised to believe that it is not polite to be angry, but it is okay to worry. This twisted logic causes us to deny being angry. Without awareness of the true meaning of our thoughts, there is not much chance of correcting the problem.

I read an article that cited figures from the American Psychological Association's Journal of Consulting and Clinical Psychology on the number of professional sessions required to correct certain psychological problems. Worry was at the top of the list. Psychotherapy helps with all ailments in an average of 58 sessions. Worry takes the largest span of time—120 sessions. That translates to more than two years of weekly sessions. Seeing those figures made me appreciate the fact that Recovery, Inc. training has taught me to handle worry (fear) thoughts as they originate.

So many techniques focus on controlling worry. In my opinion that is not healthy. Control means to repress and restrict. One of the recommended techniques to *control* worry during the day is to set aside "time to worry." I see shoving your worries in a trunk and obsessing on them later, as reinforcing fear, not removing it. Recovery, Inc. methods teach you the skills to solve problems instead of worrying about them.

I remember thinking I was better than some people because I worried more than they did. Now I see how distorted that kind of thinking really is. Worry is not a badge of honor. It is a sign of unhealthy thinking and fear.

Worry is caused by light-weight trivial affairs and heavy weight issues. Of course, if you are a *worry wart*, everything is a major issue. You believe in problems. I used to worry about many things—my car, the bills, my house, most material things. Old things and new things: how long would they last? I was uneasy about traffic, getting lost and having to ask for directions; going anywhere and getting there on time. I let planning escalate to preoccupation. Now I know I can do a certain amount of preparation and let go. Whatever unknown enters my future, I am prepared.

Worry is a negative guessing game. A game with cards marked "What if...," and "I wonder..." Some of us live our lives engrossed in the game. "What if I can't get a taxi? What if my house catches on fire? What if I get a spot on my shirt before my presentation? I wonder if I passed today's quiz? I wonder if I will feel well enough to go to the store tomorrow?"

When you catch yourself fearful or worrying, know the preoccupation is caused by your thoughts. You can change your thoughts by spotting the *possibilities and probabilities*. How likely is it that what you are dreading will come true? The ultimate tool to eliminate worry is a simple realistic fact: the only thing you really *know, is that you don't know* what is going to happen. Socrates, the Greek philosopher, said it this way: "I know, that I know not."

Very few mortals possess extraordinary telepathic powers to accurately predict the future. So when you worry, repeat the phrase, "I don't know," as many times as necessary. Every time you catch yourself thinking "What if..." Each of your "What if..." and "I wonder..." statements feed the cycle of fear. You can starve your fear and worry with, "I don't know."

Don't become upset by what you don't know! To "not know" is *not* a frightening thought. It is a fact. There are many times when there is nothing you can do about a given situation. Then, do nothing. Doing nothing is acceptable.

Although I did a fair job of eliminating worry from my everyday life, my great test came when my mother was diagnosed with terminal cancer. During her first hospitalization I visited mother daily. At the time, I also attended a full-time day class, three evening college classes, and led a Recovery meeting on another night. As a result of worry and my hectic schedule, my health started to go down hill. I suffered from recurring headaches and a constant queasy stomach. I had to make some changes in my inner environment. I had to drop my *excessive sense of responsibility*. The operative word in that statement is "excessive." I did not stop being a caring and responsible daughter. I stopped demanding so much of myself and stopped running myself ragged. I permitted myself to miss a class, or skip a visit to the hospital. I didn't have to do it *all*. When I slowed down, I looked at the facts: other members of the immediate family were at mother's side every day, she had good medical care, and I did not know what the future would bring.

Recovery, Inc. principles stand for balance in life: balance as emotional stability and balanced actions and reactions. It means being kind and gentle to yourself and others. Life is not a 50/50 proposition. At times we do give more and that is reality. You can only give without hurt and resentment when you feel your needs are being met. And you are ultimately responsible for taking care of your own needs. You can learn to be loving and caring without sacrificing yourself. You will have the energy to tackle anything you want. When you are consumed by worry, you cannot be of service to anyone, especially yourself. Consideration for what is going on with a loved one is healthy. Worry, jumping into someone else's problems, is unhealthy.

I have never attended a Toughlove group, but from what I have read, an excessive sense of responsibility sounds like what they are working on (in addition to anxieties, anger and fear). I suspect the theme for caregiver support is the same. You do get burned out when you give too much and don't take care of yourself.

An overactive sense of responsibility is not always an outcome of major life events. It can manifest itself in everyday life. It goes hand in hand with being a perfectionist, trying to be outstanding. I know mothers who iron their college-age children's clothes, all of them including t-shirts, then complain that they have no time for themselves. If you choose to perform a service for someone, don't be a martyr and complain about it.

Often worry is equated with caring for someone. It is a common misinterpretation I subscribed to. I used to believe statements similar to: "We wouldn't worry if we didn't love" and, "You are not worried, because you don't care what happens." How absurd those statements sound to me now. Are you afraid to care for yourself more than for someone you love? I remind anyone who is still in that mode of thinking, it is impossible to remain loving, supportive, reassuring and genuinely helpful unless you stay healthy and keep your own sanity.

There are times that we have to take command and shoulder extra responsibilities in family and work life. Expressing concerns and taking action as a parent, adult child or employee is part of being a responsible person. But, there is a definite difference between caring and stepping in and taking over at every opportunity.

So many people believe they can't stop worrying, especially if there is a major life event on their horizon. Perhaps the actual act of selling or buying a house is not in the realm of a triviality, but there are certainly hundreds of average irritations, frustrations and disappointments to work on during the process; many chances to seek out the fear and anger that are perpetuating an elevated stress level. The outstanding drawback of worry (fear) is that it hampers our ability to recognize we have choices. Worry is useless because it does not change results. Remember, you are in charge of your mind games, and you decide who wins.

It is the same with all life events which some people choose to label traumatic or high on the stress-scale. You can decide whether you stay inclined to react with temper (fear and anger), and let most events bother you in one way or another. Or you can carry on and view life's challenges as exercises to improve your mental fitness. You either see the events as chances to practice what you know, or wallow in misery. You *can* replace the insecure thought, "I won't make it through," to "*I can* make it through." You do not have to believe it, think it. The belief is the last to come.

When you are plagued by worry, you not only wear yourself down, but also those close to you. How can you stop the worry cycle forever? First, drop the word "worry" from your vocabulary. Replace it with "concern." You may think changing the word from worry to concern is only semantics. Right! It is. But that is the point. Worry denotes a condition which is out of your control. Concern has restraints. You control worry with one simple technique, changing thoughts. I do not believe in "constructive worry" which produces "good stress." I see worry as a beam of light in a never ending cosmos, out of my control. I see concern as the light from a candle, that I can extinguish at will.

Yes, it is correct to be concerned about a health problem, and go to a doctor. It is also good to be concerned about screechy brakes, and take the car to an auto-repair shop. Waiting for your doctor to call with the results of lab tests can be unnerving. When the "what if...," fear thoughts pop into your mind, change them to "I don't know." Worry produces confusion and muddles your thinking to the point where you don't know what to do. Concern keeps you thinking clear and rouses you to take action. It promotes rational thinking.

If you misplace an item and that item is important, worry causes you to think, "Well, what should I do now." Concern prompts you to do the common sense thing, find it, buy another, or go without the item. If something needs repair, fix it or buy a new one. It is simple. I admit, I used to find it maddening to listen to rational, practical advice like this. Now I find it so logical. Since I stopped putting so much energy into worry, I have more time for the pleasant things—such as life.

Occasionally I still have lessons on fear and worry. I travel frequently and am quite comfortable flying in a plane. Recently I was on a flight that became so bumpy the beverage cart tipped and the contents showered some passengers. It was a clear evening and I was not thrilled when the captain announced that he did not know the cause of the disturbance in the atmosphere. He finally labeled it clear-air turbulence and ordered the flight attendants to be seated. I was quite frightened and started repeating, "This is distressing, but not dangerous." My brain shot back, "But it *could* be dangerous." I countered with, "But at this *present moment* it is not dangerous." I took the time to diffuse the "what if" worry thoughts and arrived at my destination calm and collected, instead of shaky and agitated.

Post-event pre-occupation with danger is common. If your car is side-swiped and no one incurs any physical injuries, you may be caught up with worry thinking the incident *could* have been life threatening. In order to stop the train of runaway thoughts, you have to realize that the incident is over, and it was not life threatening. Be watchful that you don't attach danger after the fact.

If you find yourself with a case of insomnia because of worry or your sleeplessness starts to cause worry, try Recovery, Inc.'s prescription for sleeplessness and restless nights. It is much different from most others. Instead of getting up, stay in bed. Curb your impulse to toss around. Command your muscles to remain still in one position. You will fall asleep. If you insist you never sleep, be on guard for the tail end of dreams. They are proof you have nodded off.

Unless you have a rare physical condition, you will not become sleep depraved. The fact that you cannot fall asleep is *distressing, but not dangerous*. By lying still, your body will get some rest, and you will be able to function the next day.

Once you begin to identify your fear thoughts and handle them as they emerge, worry and sleepless nights will become a thing of the past.

27. *The PRIMARY Formula*

This is my list of basic mental fitness tools—the fundamental formula I use to feel more peaceful and comfortable, regardless of what triggers my unrest.

To eliminate feeling insecure or unsafe (fear):
— "The situation is distressing but not dangerous; it is a triviality compared to my mental health; it is average."
— "My feelings and sensations are average; they are distressing but not dangerous."

To eliminate the judgement that I am wrong (fear):
— "I am not wrong, I am average."

To eliminate the judgement someone else is wrong (anger):
— "The other person is not wrong, he or she is average; I cannot control outer environment."

To STOP impulses to inappropriate action:
— Control specific muscle groups.

To STOP apprehension or procrastination:
— Command specific muscles to move.

To STOP rushing:
— Command the muscles to slow the pace of the action.

To boost self-esteem:
— Endorse for the Effort! (not the outcome).

The primary strategy of the Method is to identify and neutralize fear and anger by replacing insecure thoughts with secure thoughts, and commanding muscles. You can custom design your own list of "*Things to Remember*" by adding any of the other pertinent phrases from the glossary (239-247).

If you make the decision to attend Recovery, Inc. group meetings to gain more knowledge and reinforce what you have learned in this book, do attend regularly. Set a goal. Commit six months or a year to your mental fitness. One two-hour meeting for 52 weeks, equals only 104 hours. That is less than 4.5 days out of 365 to devote to learning how to train your brain. Aren't you worth it? Of course you are! There should be no other answer. I know you are worth it!

The reality is, you can't receive or give support if you are not at a meeting. Be there to listen and learn, practice and grow. When individuals make efforts to gain health and peace, they do. I have witnessed the process too many times to doubt it. If you have attended meetings in the past and continue to have problems, I encourage you to attend again. Whether you went to one meeting or a year's worth, there is more you can learn. Stick to it. You can do nothing but benefit.

There are a host of excuses for not attending meetings: they are far away or on the wrong day; the leader is too old or too young; if the leader is female, the person prefers a male. Some people will not attend because they don't like the leader's personality. My response to that reasoning is: the primary goal in attending is to gain knowledge, the social aspect is secondary and optional. I encourage people to set aside their prejudices (excuses). When you look at it realistically, two hours a week is no time at all. Most of us spend 10 times as many hours per week at work or involved in other activities dealing with people we don't really consider cherished friends. And keep in mind, the Method is all about dealing with anger and fear. Weekly group meetings could be an excellent place to start working on a transformation.

Part Six

Unlocking Limits

28. *Beyond Basic Training*

Using the basics of the Recovery, Inc. system has caused a complete shift in my thinking. I have been grounded in reality training for many years and it is easier for me to accept the facts of living in this world.

As far as human relationships, I know none are permanent. Individuals drift in and out of my life all the time. Some remain friends and acquaintances for years, some for only months. I only spend a few moments with some special people. What happens here on earth is not forever. When I no longer have close or frequent contact with someone I enjoy and appreciate, I am sad—a small and normal response. If it is a more permanent loss and someone I love, I am sad and grieve—the original response plus an after-effect. I work hard at not becoming overwhelmed and distraught, at not allowing the after-effect to *consume* me. What good would it do me? None. The only purpose it would serve is to make me frantic and sick, in body and mind. I cannot afford to stay in a vicious cycle of sadness and second guessing. I have come to recognize I will never fully understand why certain things happen.

Grieving is difficult. But, there is no value in grieving a loss to the point that it makes you sick. It does not prove you loved that person who is no longer a part of your life. If you expect to go on living, you have to maintain a healthy mind and body. Pain and caring are not synonyms. You can be caring and feeling and mentally fit.

There are times when I have contact with people I do not particularly enjoy. As a realist I know it is acceptable for me not to like everyone I come in contact with, and some people I meet will dislike me. I can look at my least favorite people from the perspective that they, too, are my teachers. I may only see qualities that I do not want to adopt.

There are no mysteries to successful relationships. Neutralize fear and anger and all that remain are love and respect. And, you cannot lose your identity in a relationship when you attend to your own self-respect and inner peace.

So much of what I do and how I live today is an outgrowth of my basic-training in the program. Recovery, Inc. taught me to choose my words wisely. I have made the choice to eliminate more than the ones recommended by the program. For example, the terms Rejection, Impossible, Failure, Chaos and Crisis are not in my vocabulary. For me, there is no failure. If I attempt anything and the results are not as expected, I forge ahead and try again, sometimes more determined, sometimes less. Because I do not look back, (the past is out of my control), I maintain forward, positive motion. I choose to be optimistic.

If you want to eliminate failure from your world, make a firm decision not to speak the word "failure" aloud. Because you use words that are familiar to you, the next time you want to use the word "failure," it will take some mental exercise to reorganize your thoughts before you speak them. Use the same basic process of changing thoughts mentioned early in this book. Once you stop using the word in conversations, it will be easier to eliminate it from your thoughts. If you want to add some conscious, definitive action to your firm decision, write the letters F-A-I-L-U-R-E on a piece of paper. Then either erase it, white it out, or scribble over it to make it illegible. This physical act will reinforce your decision to wipe the word out of your vocabulary and your inner consciousness.

"Should" is another word that no longer graces my lips. There are no more "I should's," or "You should's," when you stop judging right and wrong. "I should," means I am wrong if I don't. And, "You should," means you are wrong if you don't. When you replace "should" with "could," you take away judgement and open your mind to more options. And incidentally, more inner peace.

When you use the fundamentals taught in Recovery, Inc., anything you choose to work at will become a reality in your life. I stretched beyond the primary aims of the program by using the same tools taught in it.

My training has also helped me become realistic about the days of the year that society has taught us are special: Valentine's day, my birthday, Thanksgiving, Christmas holidays, etc. I used to have very high standards about how each one of those days "should" be celebrated. I became melodramatic if the outcome was not as I expected. Now I treat everyday of my life as special and unique.

Accepting reality and seeing the positives in your life will bring you peace.

29. *A Spiritual Perspective*

Some people are disappointed in the fact that Recovery, Inc. isn't more spiritually oriented. I believe no religious aspect exists because there are unknowns in the world of theology. Dr. Low was a disciple of science. He formed, tested, and proved numerous techniques. He based his system on the valid, provable scientific truths available from his research.

Religious beliefs are not a topic of conversation and there is no formal prayer at weekly meetings. But, many individuals who attend Recovery, Inc. are on a private spiritual path. We often thank the God of our belief for sending Recovery, Inc. into our lives.

In my own experience, the spiritual side of me could not start growing until my mental side was aligned and in balance. Because of the training I received in Recovery, Inc. philosophies, today I find my spiritual path less complicated. Recovery, Inc. teachings can be construed as spiritual principles in your heart, if that is how you choose to regard them. I see them as universal life principles.

At a seminar Gary Zukav, author of *Seat of the Soul*, remarked that "Spiritual, psychological and emotional growth are ALL tied together." I know he is right. I would not be as far on my spiritual road to peace without the solid understanding of *how to* relinquish the habit of judging myself and others.

Criticizing, condemning and complaining are barriers to love. You can only give love when you liberate yourself from anger and fear. Unconditional love means accepting people for who they are, allowing them to be their own average. The Recovery, Inc. program is excellent for anyone who wants to enhance their personal or spiritual relationship with themselves and others.

Long ago I read the statement, "You can only love someone if you love yourself first." At the time I wondered,

221

"How do you learn to love yourself?" I didn't have a clue! My unrealistic perfectionist standards caused me to constantly criticize and condemn. My Recovery, Inc. training taught me how to recognize trivialities, to stop blowing things out of proportion. The concept of averageness taught me excuse myself, and others. Dropping the judgement of right and wrong in trivial every day events is the first step in learning to love. Self-endorsement also helped me create a new self-image.

More recently I've read that "You can't give, what you don't have in your heart." Because I have reached a state of self-acceptance, I have self-love. And because of the love that resides in me, in my inner-environment, I am able to share that love with others, in my outer environment.

Although I have a personal relationship with my God, the Spirit, the Universe, I know that trust in a supreme being does not exempt me from responsibility. My relationship with my Creator is a partnership—we are co-creators. Each and every one of us has choices, to hold on to the thoughts and actions that limit us, or to change, heal and grow. If you are on a spiritual journey, perhaps the God of your understanding has sent you the information in this book as a gift—the knowledge to gain new perspective on daily life.

The Recovery, Inc. Method can serve you no matter what your culture, religion, belief, or non-belief. These are human peace principles, human wellness principles.

30. *Stigma—*
The Roadblock To Freedom And Health

Shame and guilt about mental health issues are less of a barrier today than in earlier times, but are still too prevalent around the world. I speak from experience when I say that lack of education on the subject causes feelings of failure and loss of self-esteem. Humiliation may cause you to overlook your depression, anxiety, fears and anger. Stigma makes you think that perhaps your problem will just "go away." The reality is, these feelings will not disappear. When the next bout occurs, it will be worse. It is not because you are weak-minded. It is because you don't know what to do to help yourself. If you are in pain, please do not ignore it. Don't let a false sense of pride get in the way of healing.

I have talked to hundreds of people with mental health challenges, in person, by phone and at hospital after-care groups. If I calculated the total number of inquiries to Recovery, Inc., the numbers would be staggering. People reach out, yet they fear to take the actual step of attending a group meeting or seeing a professional. They collect informational material, read it, and tuck it in a drawer for later. They dial the phone number of the mental health clinic, and hang up before someone answers. They make appointments to see a professional, then cancel. The biggest reason for their apprehension is stigma.

Not many people picture high-functioning persons and mental health problems in the same frame. They have a trace of information and understanding about a diagnosis, but none about the patient. The public sees only one profile of people with mental problems—a person who harms himself or herself, or someone else. The truth is that the most common tendency is to withdraw, not attack.

Unfortunately when a mental health problem hits, it catches a person unaware and uneducated. I knew nothing about panic attacks and depression before I experienced them. I didn't know people could be afraid to drive, afraid to walk out of their house, afraid to go to the supermarket. And, I certainly did not know I could get well again. Having a mental problem does not mean you are unbalanced, deranged or crazy. It simply means you have a condition, a very treatable one.

People are treatment-shy because they do not want psychological problems on their records. Yet, most would not hesitate going for help for a physical condition. It is bad enough when the victim doesn't want to go for help, but a thousand times worse when they are held back by a relative who is afraid of tarnishing the family name.

You would not think of going through life with a broken arm dangling at a twisted angle. You would get it fixed. You would go through the discomfort of a cast, even surgery, because you know the bone could be set, mend, and be functional once it healed.

The same is true for mental disorders. You can be treated, heal and function as good or better than before. People with mental health difficulties are not irresponsible, we make improvements every day. There are survivors out there. You just haven't met them. We blend in so well, you can't even tell we have had problems, unless we tell you.

Most of us hesitate to be open about our difficulties because we're afraid others will watch our behavior for tell-tale signs. I was once very selective about who I spoke to about my illness, until I realized who I was in the past, was not who I am in the present. I found it very freeing to step out of my personal shadow. Once people knew of my past, I wasn't afraid of their finding out.

Erasing my personal stigma was a deliberate effort. I did a reality check. Dr. Low wisely included a step in the example process which illustrates how a person would have reacted before Recovery, Inc. training. I took that to another level. Instead of looking in only one area, I took a panoramic view of my abilities. At the time I was going to self-help meetings, learning, practicing and improving;

driving, working and going to school; taking part in so many activities I only dreamed about before Recovery, Inc. Reviewing the list of what I could do, made me realize I wasn't the person I used to be. I changed my focus from my illness to my wellness. I changed my belief by changing my thoughts. I could talk candidly about the old me, because I believe in the new me. Today, I don't observe my wellness. I celebrate it.

"Once mentally ill, always mentally ill," is simply not true. You can regain mental health and attain a state which is better than your old "normal." After reading this book you can say you know at least one survivor. And after working the Method for yourself, you can say you know two survivors.

Having a mental health problem is still talked about in whispers, as alcoholism was a few decades ago. Public opinion has shifted because there has been enough information published on drug dependence and enough everyday people have stepped forward to tell others of their success. Persons with addictive illnesses are not weak. Neither are people with mental illnesses. Given the correct information, people do become self-directed, and make tremendous strides in healing.

We need a massive transfer of information to the public regarding mental health treatment. The most outstanding service message I have seen is the phrase coined by the National Mental Health Association: "Depression — It's an Illness, Not a Weakness." I applaud the person who wrote the slogan, and the organization for its efforts at lifting the veils of ignorance.

I would like to hear everyone in the world respond to the question, "What is depression?" with the answer, "It's an illness." We need to start teaching that truth at grade-school level, so we do not mislead another generation.

One of the difficulties in public education efforts is that the media, local to national, hesitate to publicize mental health. I have contacted the local media in my city numerous times, and they have yet to do a story. I know for a fact that our local Mental Health Association has the same dilemma. There is no sensationalism in wellness, only in illness. Various types of media hesitate to do success stories. That reluctance is an obstacle to progress and public education.

Did you know that May is Mental Health Month, and has been since the late 1960's? Did you know that the first week in October is Mental Illness Awareness Week? This information is as obscure as National Pickle Week is to most people.

I urge the clergy and pastoral counselors to learn more about mental health. Often they are the first support people an individual with mental health problems dares to speak to. There was a time when I was so anxious sitting in church that I couldn't pay attention to the service. I could only concentrate on the terror I was feeling inside. Then I started feeling so panicky, I couldn't leave my house, no matter how much I prayed. My mind had to heal before I was aware of spiritual light.

I urge every church, synagogue, mosque and temple in every part of the world to set aside at least one day a year to talk about mental health and the importance of treatment. Mental health is a key component of spiritual health and healing. If you are a religious leader, you know that individuals in your congregation look up to you for guidance. It is important to minister to the needs of the entire person. Let people know *you* have no stigma. Let them know that it is all right to have a problem. Let them know they can and should seek help. Your message may encourage someone to reach out and become whole again.

I also have a message for mental hospital administrators and their Boards. If you want to help eliminate the stigma of mental illness, change the name of your hospital from XYZ Mental Hospital to XYZ Mental Health Hospital. The general public will start looking at your facility as a place to improve, not a place to be committed and labeled "crazy." Your clients will EXPECT to recover.

Many people cling to the misbelief a mental disorder only strikes someone who is incompetent. Others are smart enough to know they are as vulnerable as the next person. That is the real reason people are afraid to talk about anything referring to mental health. It is similar to avoiding conversations about cancer. Have you ever felt uncomfortable, or refused to talk to a person who is undergoing cancer treatment, or to one of their relatives? Very often we are uncomfortable because we do not want to think of ourselves in their shoes. Major illness can be a delicate subject.

After-the-fact stigma is just as strong. An individual I met in one of the after-care groups brought up the question, "How am I going to face my family and friends and co-workers after a stay in the hospital psych ward?" First, it is average to be concerned. The thoughts are very natural. They are distressing, but not dangerous. Spotting that secure thought will help keep the insecure ones from eating away at you. The thoughts will come back until you finally do return to work and face people. The more you talk about the event, the easier and easier it will become. If there are times when you are tired of telling the story or simply don't want to, control your speech muscles. There is no right or wrong. You do not need to tell the entire story and you do not owe everyone an explanation. Are you compelled to tell it "all" because you want to convince others you really are okay? Take this secure thought: the people who genuinely care about you, are proud you sought help. Be proud of yourself, and endorse yourself for all of your efforts. "You are doing good."

Untreated mental disorders cause dysfunction in a person and in a family. When you live through an illness, it is normal to be afraid, confused and discouraged. But remember, there are no hopeless cases. Many times in my childhood I was told I couldn't do something. Although it was permission that was being denied, I somehow converted the interpretation into "I can't—I am not capable of doing it." Maybe you are feeling "you can't."

If you know you are troubled, it is likely you will try to hide it. I encourage you to reach out. The difficulties you are facing are not rare. They are common and treatable.

Don't forgo the support that is available. Other people are not in our lives merely for decoration. Build a support network. Recovery, Inc. is out there and so are a lot of other good resources. Seeking help is a sign of maturity and emotional strength.

Touch the life of someone who is struggling with life. Tell them about the Recovery, Inc. system for mental fitness.

31. *Mind And Body*

In my mind Dr. Abraham Low was a genius, light years ahead of his colleagues at the time. Some of the personal, life-management techniques he developed are just now becoming popular. I believe that the more the public accepts and understands self-help, the more enlightened and educated they will become about mind/body healing. The knowledge is sure to ignite more interest in self-directed care.

Unfortunately, the professional mental health world reinforces the notion you will never "be yourself again." Every single day, doctors tell countless patients and families that persons with mental problems will never be "normal" again. I have heard many people say, "My doctor told me I will never be rid of obsessive thinking." These professionals are being honest, in the sense they are communicating what they know to be true. Their opinions and diagnoses are the result of studies of mental illnesses. They have facts to back them up. As the medical community did for so many years, studies and research are conducted on illness.

I am not, in any way, trying to say this is wrong. I am saying, this is the way it is. I respect the advances made in the field of mental health in the last hundred years. We are a long way from imprisoning patients and putting them in shackles.

Doctors will not be willing to tell a patient they CAN "return to normal," until someone becomes interested enough to study mental health and learn what the "winning combination" is for the survivors of mental disorders. Many practitioners will not even tell a patient or family that there is a "good chance" of beating the odds; that "some" people do survive and live useful, happy and productive lives despite a serious diagnosis. They do not want to give false hope. They believe the hope is false because they do not have scientific proof. The numbers are not there to back their statements.

What we need in the mental health world is a forward thinking "Bernie Siegel." Bernie S. Siegel, M.D., revolutionized the treatment of cancer patients. He is a surgeon who turned his curiosity about cancer survivors into a method. He researched the "survivors," the ones who beat the odds. He found that patients can consciously contribute to their wellness process and make major life improvements.

Dr. Siegel's new beliefs counter most of his formal training. Even today, despite his successes, I am sure he faces disapproval from some of the mainstream medical community. I don't think, however, he is concerned with other people's opinions. I suspect Bernie Siegel not only believes that given the right tools and techniques, humans have the ability to change their lives. He knows it.

I heard a professional comment that "going to a self-help group was part of the denial process," not accepting the diagnosis of a mental problem. I think not, Mr. Professional! Practicing self-help is NOT denial. Practicing self-help IS an *indispensable* part of self-acceptance and self-responsibility. Patients make tremendous advances in self-help groups such as Recovery, Inc., those that provide treatment as well as preventive strategies. *There are no hopeless cases.*

Professionals who oppose self-help of any kind need to realize that we can accept a diagnosis, but we do not have to accept a bleak, pessimistic, dire prognosis. I do not advocate a complete turn away from conventional treatments. But, I do believe in providing people with choices. Self-help can be viewed as an additional treatment source, not merely as an alternative one.

In the last decade we have seen tremendous acceptance in the area of mind/body medicine. Being human means having a body and a mind. Body and mind are not self-contained material objects and are no longer being studied as separate entities. The stress we feel in today's world is not the result of physical, but of mental exertion. More and more practitioners are accepting the reality that the mind and body are integrally connected.

It is interesting that the world is awakening to the mind/body connection, and Recovery, Inc. has already proved the importance of cognitive (mind) behavioral (body) therapy. What is more cognitive/behavioral and mind/body oriented than a method whose main actions are to "change thoughts" and "command muscles?" It is not a coincidence that Dr. Low's Recovery, Inc. Method is still alive and well today, despite his death in 1954.

Self-help is still viewed as a non-conformist mode of treatment. The world needs at least one professional who will explore and be enlightened; then have the courage to back self-help mental health. Not some of the time, but all of the time. Someone who believes self-care is a valid option and recommends it on a regular basis. Someone who speaks of it with enthusiasm and knowledge, not in an "oh by the way" manner. Someone who tells their patients of the *high probability* of success when self-help is part of the treatment regimen; how a patient can play a major role in their progress. Someone who prescribes self-help treatment on a patient's first visit for a stress related disorder, not as a last resort. Someone who believes in the abilities of a human being as much as Abraham Low and Bernie Siegel. A professional who is daring enough to tell colleagues and the rest of the world, the value of self-directed mental health care.

32. *In-Power*

Our lives are full of change. We never know what challenges we will have to face in "Life School." The Recovery, Inc. fitness system works in all areas and at all stages of life. Practice the methods when your body and mind are upset. Taking charge of your thoughts will cause *you* to gain power and your symptoms lose power. You will create a personal aura filled with freedom and confidence.

The Recovery, Inc. system for mental fitness has provided me some of the most effective information in the world—"In-Power"—the Power to Heal and Grow. It can do the same for you.

Fill your life with experiences, not excuses!

Not long after I started writing this book I was introduced to a beautiful song entitled **Let There Be Peace on Earth**. *I have loved it from the first. These lyrics embody the very meaning of this book and my life. I embrace the message and share it with you.*

Let There Be Peace On Earth
By Jill Jackson and Sy Miller

Let there be peace on earth, and **let it begin with me**.
Let there be peace on earth, the peace that was meant to be.
With God our Creator, children all are we.
Let us walk with each other, in perfect harmony.
Let peace begin with me, let this be the moment now.
With every step I take, let this be my solemn vow.
To take each moment, and live each moment, in peace eternally.
Let there be peace on earth, and **let it begin with me**.

Printed with permission. Jan-Lee Music © 1955, © Renewed 1983

References:

Low, Abraham A.: *Mental Health Through Will Training, A System of Self-Help in Psychotherapy As Practiced by Recovery, Incorporated*, 2nd ed., Copyright © 1952, Abraham A. Low, Copyright renewed © 1978 by Phyllis Low Cameron and Marilyn Low Schmitt.

Low, Abraham A.: *Selections From Dr. Low's Works*, Copyright © 1950, Abraham A. Low, M.D., Copyright © 1952, 1966, Mae Low.

Resource List:

Recovery, Incorporated® is a non-profit organization dedicated to the improvement of mental health. Group meetings are open to the public. Donations are requested, not required. For information on group meeting locations, Dr. Abraham A. Low's books and audio-tape lectures, please contact the International Headquarters.

Recovery, Inc., Self-Help Mental Health
802 North Dearborn Street
Chicago, IL 60610
Phone: (312) 337-5661   Fax: (312) 337-5756
www.recovery-inc.com

*****

For educational materials regarding emotional and mental health challenges and their treatment please contact:

National Mental Health Association (NMHA)
2001 N. Beauregard Street, 12th Floor
Alexandria, VA 22311
Mental Health Resource Center: (800) 969-NMHA
TTY Line: (800) 433-5959
www.nmha.org

The National Mental Health Association sponsors several free annual screening programs on mental health challenges. For information about screening locations, please contact your local Mental Health Association (MHA) or call the NMHA at the number listed above.

*****

National Institute of Mental Health
6001 Executive Boulevard, Rm. 8184, MSC 9663
Bethesda, MD 20892-9663
Voice: (301) 443-4513: Fax: (301) 443-4279:
TTY: (301) 443-8431
www.nihm.nih.gov

*****

The Abraham A. Low Institute is a non-profit organization whose mission is, in part, to apply Dr. Low's concepts and techniques to current mental health issues, and to educate the public, and inform professionals about his works.

Abraham A. Low Institute
550 Frontage Road
Suite 2797
Northfield, IL 60093
Phone: (847) 441-0445   Fax: (847) 441-0446
www.lowinstitute.org

Glossary

After-effect - fearful and angry thoughts that feed a vicious cycle.

All-absorbing purpose - a passion to do everything possible to attain "peace of mind"; a total effort: intent combined with action, desire coupled with determination.

Anger is intellectual blindness to the other person's point of view - there is invariably another side to the story; you can't see it when you are angry.

Angry temper - placing the blame on someone else for something they said, did, or did not do.

Average - typical/normal/unexceptional. Nervous symptoms are average, universal to human beings. Situations are average, the same event has happened to someone else. People are average, between the two extremes of inferior and superior.

Average original response - typical reaction.

Balance - emotional stability; balanced actions and reactions: the realist in us regulates our thinking and behavior, we have hopes, dreams and goals, acquire knowledge and use it wisely.

Bear the discomfort and comfort will come - do something enough times and you will be comfortable; there IS light at the end of the tunnel.

Belief is the last to come - you don't need to understand the principles to see results, but you do need to use the simple spotting phrases; you will be a true believer when you see them work for you.

Build up nerve resistance - by facing fear you create tolerance and immunity to it.

Business not a game - keep mental fitness at the top of your list of goals; do not gamble with your health.

Calm begets calm - work at composing yourself and it will have a ripple effect.

Change thoughts - reject and replace thoughts.

Choice of two discomforts - either brave what has to be faced and be uncomfortable, or hide from it and mentally kick yourself for not facing the fear.

Comfort is a want and not a need - you do not have to be perfectly comfortable in order to function.

Command muscles - send orders to muscles: to stop an impulse, or to move when you are apprehensive.

Cooling off period - take some time to calm down and collect yourself.

Courage to make mistakes - be brave enough to try, so what if the results are not perfect.

Discomfort - a generic, all-encompassing term for uncomfortable feelings and sensations.

Distressing but not dangerous -it feels frightening, threatening or terrifying (scary), but it really is not.

Don't strike your muscles with fear and expect them to act with precision - muscles will hesitate to carry out your commands when your brain is sending out fear messages.

Do the thing you fear or care not to do - acknowledge your feelings of fear and apprehension, and move through them.

Endorse for effort not the outcome - give yourself a pat on the back for the energy you are putting forth, not the results of what you do.

Endorsement (self) - a mental pat on the back, to you from you.

Everyday life is full of irritations, frustrations and disappointments - a fact of life in an imperfect world; anything that is upsetting you can fit into one of those categories (or all three).

Every act of self-control, produces a sense of self-respect - each time you command your muscles *not* to act and you do control an impulse, is *proof* you are indeed in control. Each case of impulse control is a small step towards building the *belief* "you are the master," in control of your body and your mind.

Excessive sense of responsibility - an extreme sense of duty and obligation towards others.

Excuse rather than accuse - release the judgement of right and wrong.

Expectations and disappointments - a fact of life; assuming results will be one way and being discouraged, dissatisfied and disillusioned when they do not turn out as planned.

Express your feelings, suppress your temper - speak what you feel in an even-tempered way.

Face, tolerate and endure the discomfort - face up to feelings; don't run from something because it may be uncomfortable.

Fearful anticipation - expecting the unpleasant or the worst.

Fearful temper - judging yourself wrong for something you said or thought; did or did not do; thinking you are not up to par with the rest of humanity.

Fear of mental collapse - fear of going "crazy," or never being "normal."

Fear of physical collapse - fear of passing out or dying.

Fear of social reputation - being afraid of what other people may think of you.

Fear of the permanent handicap - fear of never leading a "normal" life.

Fear of the Unknown - the fear of discomfort; simply being afraid of feeling afraid.

Features and gestures speak - your body language can show you are angry or fearful.

Feelings are not facts; they lie and deceive us and tell us of truths that are not there - false conclusions resulting from something that only appears to be real.

Feelings fall and run their course - work on changing thoughts or controlling muscles, then feelings and sensations will change; they are not permanent.

(a) **Firm decision steadies you** - reviewing choices is healthy, not being able to make up your mind in everyday matters keeps you tense.

Five-minute phone call - between meeting support mechanism.

(the) Goal is peace in my inner environment / bonus of peace in the outer environment - if you don't add anger and negative energy to a situation, what is happening around you may be less stormy.

Group-minded - think about your behavior with regard to the people around you; living life in a fashion which creates peace for you and those around you.

(an) Insincere gesture of friendliness, is more beneficial than a sincere gesture of hostility - a sincere act of being not-so-sincere; treating people with respect, even when you question whether they deserve that respect.

Handle each triviality as it comes along - work on each separate response of anger or fear; each irritation, frustration and disappointment.

Have your temper, but don't make an issue of it - don't create a new vicious cycle by blaming yourself for having a strong response and reacting; this does not justify anger or fear; you will not be successful in curbing your temper 100% of the time.

Helplessness is not hopelessness - you only feel helpless in a situation because you lack the knowledge of what to do; once you know, the tide can change.

Humor is our best friend, temper our worst enemy - lighten up; don't take yourself or the situation so seriously.

Imagination on fire - one thought leaping along after another; thinking about the worst possible scenario.

Immediate-effect - thoughts that follow an original response.

Impatient patient - being frustrated because you are not making the progress you think you "should" be.

Inner environment - the inner you; all that happens inside of you, the person, including your feelings and thoughts.

Inner smile - joy, light and peace at an inner level; self-pride.

Insecure thought - any negative thought is a fear thought, a threat to your basic need for safety.

Interpreting insecurely - finding only the bad or negative.

It is not how we feel, it is how we function - you *can* function even when you are uncomfortable.

It is not people, or places, or things, that give us our symptoms—it is our attitude towards them - people and things outside of us, can't make us cry, upset, feel mad, sad, crazy, unhappy or depressed; we do it to ourselves.

Keen observers and poor interpreters - adept at spying, but not so competent at picking out the real and positive.

Knowledge teaches you what to do, but practice shows you how to do it - taking knowledge and putting it to use; putting new ideas into practice to change and grow; skill comes from practice.

Know that you don't know - you can't forecast the future; very few mortals possess unusual telepathic powers.

Lowered feelings - the expression of choice for depression.

Lower your standards and your performance will rise - learn to set realistic goals and boost your productivity; convert your worry energy to problem-solving energy.

Merely a harmless outpouring of a nervous imbalance - the harmless feelings, thoughts and sensations which characterize how you react.

Muscles re-educate the brain that there is no danger - when you are apprehensive, move your muscles despite your fear. When a muscular act carries you through the fear, when you have faced it and it is behind you, it is proof you "can" do it. Your mind receives the message and imprints a new brain cell with "no danger involved."

Nervous fatigue - discouragement disguised in feeling tired.

Nervous fear is the fear of discomfort - it is not specific places or events you fear, it is the sensations.

No right or wrong in the trivialities of everyday life - as long as there are no moral or ethical issues involved, there is no explicit right or wrong.

Not giving outer expression to inner feelings - don't let your feelings rule your actions.

Not transparent - no one else can "see" how you are feeling on the inside.

Objective/objectivity - focusing on a material object in terms that can be measured and verified.

Old habit patterns - the standard thinking and behavior patterns of the past.

Original response - first response to an irritation, frustration or disappointment.

Outer environment - absolutely everything which is not within the confines of you.

Outer environment can be rude, crude and indifferent - there will always be some people who act in a less-than-considerate manner.

Part acts - facing or doing things a step at a time.

Partial view - zeroing in on one aspect, usually a negative one; not seeing the entire picture

Past practice - once you have faced a situation, you have experience; there will be less apprehension when you face the same or a similar event.

Phasic not basic - whatever it is, it is not going to last forever.

Plan, decide and act - weigh the options, make a decision, then follow through with action.

Possibilities and probabilities - how likely is it your dreaded anticipation will come true.

Pre-disposed to temper - having a tendency to anger and/or fear.

Processing - the working-up process; an after-effect filled with angry and fearful thoughts; often contains thoughts of blame and retaliation.

Racing thoughts - an avalanche of thoughts; mind chatter.

Realistic - rational; factual; not emotional.

Realistic sense of self-pride - being sincerely proud of yourself.

Replace insecure thoughts with secure thoughts - the perfect and ultimate secure thought for replacing a fear thought: "distressing but not dangerous."

Return of the symptoms, does not mean return of the illness - we never go back as far as we were - because of knowledge, insight and practice, we never go back to square one.

Romanto-intellectualist - a person who knows more and knows better; who lives in a world of dreams and fantasies and is not grounded in reality.

Sabotage - when you are able and prepared, but not willing, to put your knowledge into practice; when you do the opposite of what is good for you.

Self-appointed expectations lead to self-induced frustrations - self-designed disappointments; a pre-conceived idea things will go a certain way; hoping for unrealistic results.

Self-endorsement - a mental pat on the back, to you from you.

Self-importance being stepped on - feeling angry or fearful because someone hasn't noticed or appreciated you.

Self-led rather than symptom-led - skeptical, pessimistic fear thoughts do not have to rule your life. You regulate your thoughts.

Setbacks are average - a time of less-than-perfect progress that is part of the process.

Speech muscles - all the muscles involved in speaking.

Spot - see or notice. When you look for a friend in a crowd and finally see him, you have "spotted" him despite the swarm of other people. When you're upset, your mind is swarming with thoughts. You "spot" or "zero in" on what to correct.

Spotting techniques - simple phrases to overcome tension; rational thoughts to ground you in reality.

Symbolic or shallow victories - the temporary feeling of power, feeling alive and in charge when you rant, rave, rage, roar or go on a rampage; inevitably followed by self-blame for acting out of control.

Striving to be exceptional and fearing we are not average - trying to be a perfectionist; when you think you are not "as good as" the next person and constantly try to prove that you are acceptable.

Strong link - a circumstance, event or person that is likely to cause a response of fear and/or anger.

Suggestible - being sensitive and vulnerable.

Supreme goal - the paramount aim, good mental health.

Take the ceiling off the amount of discomfort you are willing to bear - remove the limits, you can stand it.

Take the emergency out of a situation - take out the danger that is causing the fight or flight response

Temper - fear and anger; the cause of *all* tension and stress.

Temper at the illness - being angry at having a sensitive stress receptor, and having to work hard at correcting it.

Temper blocks insight - you will not see alternatives until you crumble the barrier set up by insecure, unsafe and angry thoughts.

Temper causes tension and tension causes symptoms - fear and anger are manifested as tension, tension produces symptoms.

Temperamental deadlock - a standoff; you think you are right and the other person thinks they are right.

This is a triviality compared to my mental health - compare the importance of what is happening around you against the importance of the peace you are striving for; consider anything and everything that upsets you in the perspective your inner harmony is of prime importance; mental fitness comes first.

Total effort - intent combined with action; desire coupled with determination.

Total view - looking at the big picture will uncover the positives.

To talk it up, is to work it up - you keep negative events alive and at the forefront of your mind when you talk about them or mentally review them.

Triviality - an irritation, frustration or disappointment that is not worth getting upset or sick over.

Trust your basic functions to carry you through - confidence in the body's ability to get you through.

Try and fail, try and fail, try and succeed - the very definition of "training"; you will aim at the same goal more than once before you are successful.

Turn a cool and chilly shoulder toward the situation - a mental about-face; turn your thoughts elsewhere.

Vicious cycle - a series of fearful or angry thoughts which cause stress and tension.

Want not a need - a "nice to have," but not an absolute necessity to exist.

We get well in direct proportion to the amount of discomfort we are willing to bear - the more you step out of your comfort belt, the more you will grow.

While you are endorsing yourself, you cannot be blaming yourself - since you can only have a single thought at a time, make it a positive, secure one. (see Self-Endorsement)

(the) Will - your personal decision maker that says "yes" or "no"; it accepts or rejects your thoughts and ideas and stops or releases impulses.

Will to bear discomfort - don't avoid being uncomfortable, choose to face it. You must reach out of your safe territory to make headway.

Will to effort - be willing to exert some energy.

Working-up process - an after-effect filled with angry and fearful thoughts; often contains thoughts of blame and retaliation.

Work it down and drop it - neutralize fear/anger, and proceed with your day.

You cannot be comfortable in an uncomfortable situation - some situations are more stress-producing.

You cannot control outer environment - you only have control of yourself; you can influence and guide others, but never totally govern what they say, do, or do not do.

*****

Visit: www.pljunlimited.com
for samples of how to adapt these
versatile skills in your daily life.
Look for: *Life Skills in Action* and *What Do I Do When*

Index

abuse, 28,29
acceptance, 49,51,125,137,138,
175,221
of problem, 30,31,40,44,72,116,
129
accountability, 29,33,35
action, 12,52,57,62,64,84,96,98,
101-104,131,138,170,175,196,
210,211
addiction, 11,193
adrenaline, 74,195
after-effect, 153-155,158,168,174,
182,185-186,188,201,207,217,239
agoraphobia, 25,28,39,143
alternatives, 27,90,205,246
anger, 21,40,63,134,145-147,151,
154-159,196,197,203,205,210,213,
217,221,242,244,245,246,247
control, 126
identify, 21,145-147,151
intellectual blindness, 202,239
manage/neutralize, 181-183,185,
186,188-190,203, also see excuse
mind/body responses, 147
silent, 158,197
subtle, 151
angry temper, 145-146,239
anxiety, 11,20,22,39,40,55,72-75,
77,78,85,86,88,100,143,169,195,
196,197,224
apprehension, 42,43,46,51,59,72,
77,120,157,163,164,174,213,223,
240,243,244
arguments, 158,184, also see anger
stopping, 203
assertive, 31,123,189
attitude, 9,40,57,128,129,135,152,
167,168,173,178,179,182,197,205,
243
audience, 41
average, 50,112,113,114,119,120,
127,167,168,171,175,181-185,187,

204,210,213,221,239
awareness, 20,25,41,84,108,
146,155,174,181,207,226
back-ward patient, 28
balance, 12,56,116,131,161,169,
170,181,196,209,221,239
basic functions, 113,168,246
basic training tools, 99-100
behavior, 9,11,21,30,31,39,40,
57,67,134,146,169,181,184,186,
187,189,224,239,242,244
changing, 96,102,192,195,197,
200
unacceptable, 185,188,195
belief, 33,35,45,65,105,124,125,
157,165,166,182,194,211,225,
230,239,240
benefits, 105,158
bi-polar, 28,78
blame, 23,33-36,90,127,139,
145,151,182,192,193,239,242,
244,245,247
blocks, 10,64,205,246
body, 61,64,73,102,104,134,137,
177,182, also see mind/body
negative effects on, 21-22,67,
100-101,217
reactions, 147,152,154,155,156,
195
sensations, 25,79,115,120,128,
185
body language, 154,241
borderline personality disorder,
28
boredom, 21
boundaries, 85,87,117
brain, 61,64,77,79,100,101,102,
103,119,126,195,212,214,240,
243
business, 89,157,191,239
but if..., 203
calm, 9,19,39,73,96,99,

Index   249

Personal Notes

_____

_____

_____

_____

_____

_____

_____

_____

_____

_____

_____

_____

_____

_____

_____

_____

_____

_____

Personal Notes

Additional copies of
Peace of Body, Peace of Mind
by Rose VanSickle
may be ordered by sending
check or money order to:

PLJ Unlimited
P.O. Box 98441
Raleigh, NC 27624-8441

VISA/MC orders call:
1.800.448.6246

Visit our website at:
www.pljunlimited.com

All prices include shipping and handling:
$17.95   U.S. orders
$15.99   NC residents (includes 7% sales tax)
$23.95   Canada and all others (U.S. funds please)

Quantity discounts are available from the
publisher, PLJ Unlimited.